Amazing Grace for Fathers

Amazing Grace for Fathers

75 Stories of Faith, Hope, Inspiration, and Humor

Edited by
Jeff Cavins, Matthew Pinto,
Mark Armstrong, and Patti Maguire Armstrong

ASCENSION PRESS

West Chester, Pennsylvania

Ascension Press
Post Office Box 1990
West Chester, PA 19380
Orders: (800) 376-0520
www.ascensionpress.com

Cover design: Kinsey Caruth

Printed in the United States of America

ISBN-10: 1-932645-99-3
ISBN-13: 978-1-932645-99-6

To the unsung heros in our lives, our fathers:

Robert Cavins

Albert Pinto

Richard Armstrong

Frank Maguire

Your selfless giving to your families have shown each of us the very heart of God. Thank you for all you have done for us.

— Jeff Cavins, Matthew Pinto,
Mark Armstrong, and Patti Maguire Armstrong

Contents

Chapter 1 — **A Father's Love**

Chapter 2 — A Father's Strength

Chapter 3 — A Father's Faithfulness

Chapter 4 — **A Father's Humor**

Chapter 5 — **A Father's Wisdom**

Chapter 6 — A Father's Character

Chapter 7 — A Father's Hope

∽

Introduction

Dad. The word conjures up a variety of images depending on who is doing the imagining. For energetic four-year-old boys, Dad is the ultimate wresting partner. For six-year-old daughters, he is a security blanket. For busy moms, he is a much-needed helping hand. For testosterone-rich teenage boys, he is "the heavy," the enforcer of rules. For teenage girls, he is the measure by which she will soon seek out a husband. For the family, he is the rock, the anchor, the one who leads the way.

After secular culture seemingly disposed of fathers during the free-wheeling divorce culture of the 70s and 80s, a new-found recognition of dad's importance has occurred of late. And fathers are responding. Not only are they showing up at more kids' sporting events and parent-teacher conferences than perhaps ever before, they are making great strides in teaching their children the Bible and the traditions of the Church. They are demonstrating to their children not only the faithfulness of their heavenly Father, but also how to treat a woman, how to sacrifice, and how to be a servant.

When we read the Bible, we see that there are many things that God is "like." He is like a shepherd in Psalm 23. He is like a warrior in Jeremiah 20 and a provider in Genesis 22. There is, however, one defining word that trumps all others and wrangles every metaphor into one and that is "Father." God is a Father who is raising a family and He loves His children dearly. As a Father, God protects, He provides, He is present, and ultimately He dies for the good of His family.

The task set out for all fathers is to live in such a way that they image their heavenly Father. Think about it—God has given children a living icon in earthly fathers that will demonstrate the attributes of their heavenly Father. This book is about men who have in some way reflected God to their children. Our prayer is that you will be inspired by these stories and make that decision to become a divine mirror of our heavenly Father.

One of the best things about fathers is that they do all this with little fanfare. They are content with being in the background. This may be because of a certain ingrained passivity among fathers—a tendency to let mom take the lead with the "kid stuff"—or because every father is profoundly connected in some way with the transcendent nature of God the Father. Either way, there's a certain beauty in fathers being in the background, to respond in moments of crisis. Fathers are always ready to investigate a strange noise or late-night knock on the door or to hug a daughter blessed with overly-active emotions.

The stories in *Amazing Grace for Fathers* reflect the many faces and experiences of today's father. They show his remarkable versatility and his single-minded simplicity. They show his flaws, but also his virtues. For the most part, they reveal that, when push comes to shove, dad is always there—ready to deliver on the promise that is in his heart: to serve rather than be served.

Our culture has a tendency to view a man's value by the work he does. Yet society is now coming to see that the most important work of all is to "raise the future" in our children, and that this crucial work cannot be done without good dads. In the pages ahead, you will meet many "good dads." Their experiences and example will serve as inspiration to all fathers. Applaud them, pray for them, and encourage them. Our children, our families, and our world will be the better for it.

—Jeff Cavins, Matthew Pinto,
Mark Armstrong, and Patti Maguire Armstrong

Chapter 1

A Father's Love

9/11

Why me? It's a question often posed to God by people forced to endure hardship. Ironically, it is the exact same question often asked by people who survive a catastrophe while others die. It is the very question that haunted me after I escaped from Tower 1 of the World Trade Center in New York City on September 11, 2001.

Why me? Why did God allow me to narrowly escape and return to my family? I knew that my colleagues loved their spouses and children as much as I loved mine. But so many never had the chance to see their families again. When I returned home after the surreal terror of 9/11, embracing my wife and children and thanking God for my life were the only things that mattered to me. But why me? Why was I granted such a blessing beyond measure while so many others lost their lives and their loved ones?

I do not recall many of the details of my ride on the Long Island railroad to Manhattan that morning. I loved my job as a money market broker with Garban Intercapital, a brokerage firm, so I likely was thinking of what I was going to do at work that day. Often, I prayed a Rosary for my family. They were everything to me. Roxane and I had married in 1989. We had three children: Nicholas, age nine; Brianna, five; and the baby, Samantha, would be one in December. I grew up in a strong Catholic family. Although there had been an ebb and flow to my religious practice, once I experienced the all-encompassing love of fatherhood God became my all. Fatherhood was the core of my being now and I became painfully aware that my infinite love for my family was not enough. I could never love my children enough to fully protect them physically and spiritually. I had to do my best and then trust God for the rest.

As I stepped off the train and headed for the subway that Tuesday morning, I was greeted by a perfect fall morning. The air was crisp enough to put a jaunt in everyone's step as we headed to our destinations under a clear blue sky. I took the elevator up to the 25th floor, headed to the trading desk and quickly got on the phone with a customer amid the din of a busy trading floor. It was business as usual. Then, just before 9 a.m., a deafening explosion or some sort of impact rocked the building. I literally fell out of my chair. The building swayed like a reed but then righted itself. Outside, glass and paper showered from above. Screams pierced the air as horrified faces looked around trying to make sense out of what had just happened. My best guess was that maybe the restaurant at the top had experienced an explosion or perhaps a small helicopter had crashed into the building.

Within seconds, terrified people began evacuating. I stayed and answered the phone, explaining to another customer that something bad had just happened and we did not know what it was yet. Then, thirty seconds after the first impact, there was a second explosion. Later, I learned that after the first plane hit, jet fuel had spilled down the elevator shaft and ignited. A ball of fire careened down the shaft and exploded when it impacted the lobby. Again, the building shook. An old friend and colleague, Marie, shouted like a drill sergeant ordering everyone to get out. My boss, Nick, was the last to leave the trading desk, following right behind me.

At that point, everyone quickly began filing out. My body had stiffened but I felt no panic. That all changed when I tried to get onto the stairwell and discovered that people were packed in it like sardines. I could not even get on it. Ceiling tiles were cracking and displacing, and smoke drifted into the hallways.

For the first time, it registered that I might not get out alive. "Dear God," I pleaded. "Please let me see my family again." I frantically looked around. The elevators were not working. There was no way out. My eyes met a colleague, Oscar, who called to me.

"I know another way out," he told us and another co-worker. We gratefully followed him to a stairwell across from the men's room. It was much smaller and narrower. I had always thought it was the door to a closet. Although this stairwell was filling up, we could still get in. Relief filled me as we headed down the stairs, trusting that we would soon get out. There was even some lighthearted banter among people as we hurried down. But when I arrived at the 16th floor, the second tower was hit. No one had any idea what was going on, but we felt the impact and inhaled the smell of jet fuel. Now, it was clear that whatever was happening was no accident.

My only thoughts were prayers to God, pleading to see my family again. Yet, panic clouded my head, making prayer difficult. "I'm sorry, God," I said in frustration, struggling unsuccessfully to pray a coherent sentence. My being longed for two things: to get home in the embrace of my family and get to church in the embrace of God. I knew He was with me, but I could not mentally verbalize anything. I knew God felt my feelings and that was all I could manage. I thought of an aunt and uncle, both of who had recently died. Somehow, I felt their presence and I pleaded for their help.

When I reached the twelfth floor, a voice echoed up the stairwell, commanding us to leave. It was the fire department. My survival instincts refused to consider such an option. *There's no way I'm getting off this stairway*, I thought, fearing I'd never get back on. *It's the only way out.* No one was willing to budge. The firemen were forced to squeeze their way past us. I flattened myself onto the railing and watched the seemingly fearless lieutenant mount the steps. Behind him were a dozen young men in fire suits and helmets, carrying axes and a fire hose. Their eyes revealed something terrible but we knew not what. We absorbed their fear and the stairwell went silent. After they passed, my heart raced to a dizzying pulse. "Please God, let me get home," I begged. In my my mind, I saw my wife and children and felt their embrace. I desperately pleaded with God to get me home to them.

A woman just behind us struggled to help a man in his 60s down the stairs. He was asthmatic and the smoke that was descending had rendered him almost helpless. Another colleague, Bruce, and I each took an arm and helped him down. Water from the sprinkler system made the stairway slick, so each step to survival had to be carefully measured. But we were almost there. Finally, the door to the mezzanine level of the lobby opened like a river releasing a flood of people. The chandeliers overhead rattled and the surrounding window glass lay around us in shards. A police officer who saw us helping the older man took over. He warned us not to look around—to just get out. But it was impossible to avoid seeing the pockets of fire and charred body parts strewn about.

My mind could not process what my eyes took in. The police directed the survivors away from the building. We had to wait for a police officer, across an open-air breezeway from the North Tower to 6 World Trade Center, to call us over. He was looking up to make sure we were clear of falling debris and falling bodies. From 6 World Trade Center we went to a pedestrian highway overpass. When I got to the overpass there was a thunderous roar. People screamed. I thought to myself, "My God, not again." But it was the sound of U.S. fighter jets that had made it to the World Trade Center. Then there were crashing sounds. I looked over to my building and saw someone go crashing through the overhang. People were jumping. The police kept directing us away. We crossed the street to the World Financial Center and proceeded to the promenade on the Hudson River. Once there, I finally stopped and looked up at the towers. I could see where the impact was on Tower 1. Smoke billowed out of both towers, which now glowed red with flames. People below that impact zone were waving handkerchiefs and jumping. I saw people holding hands and jumping together. One man—who was engulfed in flames when he jumped out the window—went down in a stream of smoke. It was incomprehensible.

I was still with my boss and three colleagues as we were directed to keep moving. We were about 200 yards from Tower 1, directly west. My boss lived in New Jersey, so he told us to get on the ferry so we could all go to his house. Two ferries pulled in at that moment so we got right on. The boats filled to capacity within minutes. As the ferry pulled out, I could not take my eyes off what was happening. My boss turned his back, unable to watch. A few minutes into the trip, Tower 2 went down. Dust and debris filled the air. Lower Manhattan completely disappeared from view.

Like stricken war refugees, people were exhausted and numb, many of them crying. Our group quietly got off the ferry together and boarded the train to Nick's home in

Franklin Lakes, New Jersey. My first instinct was to reach Roxane, but the cell networks were overloaded with calls. *She's afraid I am dead,* I thought. *Dear God,* I prayed, *please comfort Roxane. Help me get through to her.*

Two hours after after we boarded the ferry, I sat with my co-workers at my boss' house. It was a beautiful day in a quiet neighborhood, as if the unimaginable nightmare we had just escaped from had never even happened. I was finally able to get through to Roxane on my cell. "Honey, I'm OK," I cried. "I'm at Nick's house." The relief of finally connecting with her opened a floodgate of emotions. Words escaped me. Roxane, too, could not speak. For many minutes, we sobbed together on the phone. Many of our friends and relatives were at our house with her. I longed to get home, but I was so grateful that we had finally made contact.

Transportation to and from the city was blocked, so it would not be until the next day that I found a way home. A cousin who was returning from business in Chicago came through to get me. When the car pulled up in front of my house late Wednesday morning, again my emotions flowed. Roxane and the kids came running out to meet me, along with my mother, mother-in-law, and other relatives. "Daddy!" my kids screamed and jumped into my arms. Hearing them say "Daddy" was the sweetest sound I had ever heard. Roxane and I sobbed as we embraced. I was overcome with gratitude to God and sheer joy at being reunited with my loved ones. I saw every aspect of my life as a priceless treasure that I had been privileged enough to return to.

I felt physically weak and mentally exhausted, but my spirit soared in the embrace of my family. I spent the day surrounded by people, crying and sharing my story. The

next day, Thursday, I wanted to take Nicholas to his school,
St. Agnes, and then attend morning Mass.

"Bye, Dad," Nicholas said, giving me a hug. But when
he pulled away and saw tears streaming down my cheeks, he
became concerned. "Are you OK, Dad?" he asked.

"Yes," I insisted. "I'm just so happy." I kissed and hugged
my precious son again and told him I would see him after
school.

I got back in the car and drove to the church entrance.
But as I walked to the church door, all my strength drained
from me. I literally needed to support myself on each pew as
I pulled myself up to the front of church. Then, I collapsed
in the front pew and cried harder than I have ever cried in
my life. All my emotions—fear, joy, thankfulness, love ...
everything—poured forth. And guilt. I had been blessed
beyond measure to be reunited with my family, but what
about all the others? Fifty members of my neighborhood
community never returned. At that point, I did not know
the numbers, but I had no doubt that those who did not
make it out had loved their family as deeply as I loved mine.
Someone from behind me rubbed my back as it shook and
heaved between sobs. They never said a word but their touch
consoled me.

Tears flowed continuously throughout Mass. Thankfully,
the priest always brought communion to those sitting in the
front pew; I would not have had the strength to get up. After
people received Holy Communion, they all made contact
with me by patting my shoulder or back, or squeezing my
hand. I did not know who they were, but I appreciated their
desire to comfort me.

After Mass, Monsignor Caldwell, the celebrant, came
over and talked with me. Through tears, I admitted that
although I had never wanted anything more in my life than
to survive, now I struggled with the question, *Why me?*

"What makes me so special?" I asked. "So many of my friends and colleagues died that day. They had young kids just like me. Why didn't they survive and I did?"

Monsignor Caldwell patted my arm. "That is something you do not need to know," he said quietly. "God has plans for you. It's not meant for you to figure out." I knew Monsignor was right. His words brought comfort, but my grief for the others was still tinged with guilt.

A couple of days later, our company set up temporary operations in another office space. Everyone was invited to return as they felt able. For the next few days, I stayed home with Roxane, playing with and reading to the kids, and helping them with their homework. Physically, I still felt weak, as if I were recovering from the flu. But by the following Wednesday, I went back to work. For weeks, the work seemed meaningless but the camaraderie was intense. We would go out for long, therapeutic lunches and share our stories and emotions with one another. I still could not completely shake the guilt, but it was reassuring to be with other friends who had survived also.

Life gradually became routine again, although it was never the same. Then, a year-and-a-half later, in April of 2003, Roxane was diagnosed with a brain tumor on her left optic nerve. An MRI revealed it was benign. On May 5, she went in for what was expected to be a routine operation, as far as brain surgery goes. The surgery lasted ten hours; three hours longer than expected, but her recovery looked good. By the following day, however, fluid began to build up on the brain and her condition became critical. The situation worsened to the point that we did not know if she would live or die. It was necessary to put her in a medically-controlled state of unconsciousness while doctors worked furiously to

control the swelling. I again prayed for survival; this time
for Roxane's.

On the day of the surgery, a priest had come to visit the
hospital. I shared my story with him and confessed that I still
carried guilt that I had survived while so many others did
not. "Don't you see," he said to me. "Who would take care
of Roxane and the kids if you were not here? Your family
needs you," he said. "God still has work for you to do."

As I stepped in and took over for my family, acceptance
and understanding grew in me. Previously, I had mentally
understood the reality of God's will, but now I was
experiencing it on a deeper level. I was here because God
still had a purpose for me in this world. It does not not mean
that those who died are not missed terribly, but it is God's
call. There is always pain and loss beyond our choosing. I do
not need to feel guilty for still being with my family. I am a
husband and a father, here at God's bidding to love and serve
those in my life.

Since 9/11, my desire to serve others has increased
tenfold—beginning with my family. God still wants me
here for that purpose. It is not for me to question, but only to
meld my will to His and bask in the blessings He gives me.

Roxane eventually made a full recovery. Our trials have
been our triumphs. Life's joys have been magnified since
our brushes with death. As for me, not a day goes by that I
don't think of 9/11 to one extent or another. I would never
had chosen to go through it, but I have grown because of
it. My thankfulness runs much deeper. I see also that it has
brought out the best in people. Immediately following the
tragedy, there was a great outpouring of love and caring. In a
city where people rarely acknowledge one another, passersby
made eye contact and greeted one another. Churches filled
and people wanted to reach out and help others in need.

When Roxane needed to be taken care of for awhile, our community rallied around us with meals, cleaning, and a multitude of other help. Our children have witnessed the response of adults. They have learned that comforting others also brings comfort to yourself.

When I recently brought Nicholas to volunteer at a soup kitchen for his confirmation volunteer hours, we both loved it. I believed in helping others before, but it's different now. Those of us who experienced 9/11 live life on a deeper level than we did before. We understand that love is what matters most. And that is a blessing.

—Michael Fineo

Michael Fineo and his family live in Rockville Centre, New York. He loves taking his three kids for bike rides and long walks with their black lab, Sonny.

Team Hoyt

I was the captain of my high school football and baseball teams, and I married my high school sweetheart, who was captain of the cheerleaders. So naturally we expected our first child to be a great athlete.

When I first saw my son, Rick, right after he was delivered, I thought he was doing push-ups. *Already an athlete,* I thought. But they were not push-ups. To my horror, I learned he was gasping for air, fighting for his life. His umbilical cord had wrapped around his neck just before delivery, nearly strangling him to death. Those push-ups were spasms as he fought to stay alive.

After running some tests, the doctors told my wife, Judy, and me that Rick would never talk or walk. "Your son will be a vegetable for the rest of his life. The best thing you could do for him now is to place him in an institution," he said.

"No," we told them. "He is our son. Rick does not belong in an institution, he belongs with us." We took Rick home and gave him the love and attention all children deserve from their mother and father. Later, we had two healthy sons, Rob and Russell.

We went everywhere as a family. All of us talked to Rick, even though he could not talk back. Rick would smile and his eyes twinkled. The doctors were skeptical, but I was convinced that something was going on upstairs in that brain of his. If only there was some way we could prove it.

Finally, when my son was twelve, we were able to show the doctors there really was someone in there. A machine was invented that allowed Rick to use the limited motion of his head to slowly type, letter by letter, a couple of words.

I thought his first words would be something like, "Hi Dad," or "Hi Mom." But Rick fooled both of us with his great sense of humor and his love of sports. "Go Bruins," he typed. At the time, the Boston Bruins were making a run for the Stanley Cup. Finally, my son could speak! The doctors had been wrong. What came next, though, was even more amazing.

Rick learned about an upcoming charity road race for a paralyzed athlete and typed out, "Dad, we need to run in that race." I was forty at the time, out of shape, and had never run more than a mile in my life. But I looked in those eyes of Rick, my son, who could not even walk. How could I say no?

I had never seen a wider smile on Rick than when we finished that five-mile race. I pushed Rick in his wheelchair and finished in second-to-last place. I was pleased with myself, thinking we had fulfilled a dream.

After the race Rick revealed to me, "Dad, when we were running in that race it felt like my disability disappeared." His words touched me deep in my heart and brought tears to my eyes.

It was not long before Rick and I were entering just about every road race New England had to offer, including the Boston Marathon over and over again. You might think the story would end there, but Rick's competitive spirit pushed Team Hoyt—as everyone was calling us by then—to new challenges.

"How about triathlons, Dad?" Rick asked one day.

Triathlons consist of swimming, biking, and running. *Well, that would be a challenge,* I thought. I couldn't swim and I had not been on a bike since I was six. But how could I say no to Rick?

In 1985, we moved to a house on a lake. My first time in the water, I sank. But soon, I could keep my head above water and learned to swim. I would tow Rick in an inflatable raft for the swimming portions of the triathlons. I had a special custom-made bike that allowed Rick to sit up front as we entered in all the triathlons we could.

Three years later, Rick's competitive nature stepped it up one more notch when we entered the most grueling of all triathlons—the "Ironman" in the tropical heat of Hawaii. It consists of a 2.6-mile swim, a 112-mile bike ride, and ends with a full marathon. With Rick's undying spirit to encourage me through, we did it.

Were the surprises over? Not by a long shot. The biggest one was still to come. Just a few months before Rick and I were scheduled to run in our 23rd straight Boston Marathon, I ran into an unexpected problem of my own. I had heart attack.

My doctor told me that my main artery was 95 percent blocked. "Dick, if you weren't in shape, you would have died fifteen years ago," I was informed.

Rick had saved my life. If not for him, I would have been a couch potato and been dead years ago. So, we are indeed a team. Having a severely-disabled child may seem like a tragedy to many, but to me, it has been a triumph. Every time we participate in a race, we transcend Rick's disabilities. I have become stronger both physically and emotionally through my son. Having Rick as my son has been a true blessing.

—Dick Hoyt

Together, Dick and Rick Hoyt established and run The Hoyt Foundation, Inc., an organization whose goal is to integrate the physically-challenged into everyday life by making the able-bodied more aware of the issues that they face. They tour the country doing motivational speaking engagements to groups and corporations to promote their motto—"Yes You Can." For more information, please visit their website www.teamhoyt.com

The Good Race Run Together

Rolling between my grandfather's index finger and thumb was not just a string of beads, but a way of life. In a dimly-lit hospital room, he gathered his children and grandchildren around the bed of my grandmother. There is strength in numbers, and in times of great difficulty we embrace each other and the rituals of the Catholic faith. My grandfather is a strong man; he never complains. A World War II veteran and retired carpenter, enduring difficulty by embracing the faith is not foreign to him. Through the weeks of long car rides to the hospital, my grandfather always made certain to begin each day with Mass and end each visit in prayer. As a college student studying only minutes away from the hospital, I was blessed with the opportunity to join my grandparents nearly every day in cherished moments of prayer and companionship.

As my grandmother's death grew nearer, my grandfather led the family in praying the glorious mysteries of the Rosary. These decades were appropriate not only for the liturgical season of Easter, but also for the moments we were yet to experience.

My father had taught me how to pray. His father had taught him. Their lives of prayer prepared me for a maturation of faith that grows from the passing of generations on through death. Their paternal nurturing helped me to understand the strength that blossoms from a faithful family. A devoted life of prayer helped prepare my family for one of life's certainties: death. Standing at the bedside of my dying grandmother with my father and grandfather, I celebrated the efficacy of the prayers and rituals of our faith.

My grandparents recognized the importance of family prayer. They raised their family on the foundation of a strong, traditional Catholic faith. For my father and his siblings, structured prayer and devotionals—in particular, the Rosary—are as familiar as the tune of "Happy Birthday."

The final hours of my grandmother's life were filled with the grace of family prayer. What was once a gathering in the living room for night prayer was now a reunion of family in a hospital room sharing the same faith. Just as it had been for years, the prayer was led by the head of the family, my grandfather.

Awaiting Grandpa's lead into the second glorious mystery, "the Ascension of Our Lord," we heard him sob. At last he spoke. "Zach, you lead us. You take the next decade." I, the youngest person present, was asked to lead the extended family in prayer at the foot of my failing grandmother, on the most difficult day of our lives. Praying for strength, I took after the example of my grandfather and led the family through the second decade. Though he was stricken with grief, I could sense the pride my father felt as I progressed through the Hail Marys. Like my grandfather, my father has taught my brothers and me the rituals that surround and support the way of living a faithful life as Catholic men. As a pillar of strength he stood alongside Grandma's hospital bed for the comfort and consolation of his family.

As my grandmother struggled for breath, my grandfather held her hand and spoke sweet words to the love of his life, "I love you, Sweetie. Thank you for all our beautiful children. Thank you for all our beautiful grandchildren. I love you, and I'm sorry for any trouble I gave you. I love you, Sweetie. I'm not far behind you."

Every exposed inch of Grandma's skin was lovingly stroked by her children and grandchildren. My grandfather held her hand with a rosary placed between them. Embraced in life, the prayers and rituals of the faith brought comfort and familiarity at the hour of Grandma's death. A chorus of "I love you" resonated from the hearts and mouths of the family. As the prayers, lead by my grandfather, were recited in unison, Grandma was called home to join the angels and saints in the song of eternal praise.

For my grandfather, the passing of his bride was made easier by the practice of the prayers and rituals of the Catholic faith, and the ability to share that faith with his children. Such is the reward of a life of prayer. My grandfather and father have handed me a baton and have encouraged me to run. It is a baton made of the strongest faith, coated with devotionals, studded with rosary beads, and with the Eucharist at its core. I have chosen to run with it, and pass it on as my grandfather has for my father, and my father has for me.

—Zachary Bennett

Zachary Bennett, a recent graduate of the College of St. Scholastica in Duluth, Minnesota, hails from Sandstone, Minnesota. He is currently discerning his vocation as a seminarian for the Diocese of Duluth. Bennett is an avid outdoorsman and enjoys sharing his faith with all.

A Baby, Not a Choice

The news hit me like a ton of bricks. I wanted a healthy son. The doctor was telling us something different. The test my wife, Sharon, had taken showed a high chance that our child might have Down Syndrome. The only way to know for sure was to go to the nearest perinatal center that specialized in diagnostic testing for birth defects. We scheduled a test and counseling for a few days later.

I squeezed Sharon's hand and said a silent prayer. We were both in our mid-thirties and had a healthy baby girl, Alex, just the year before. Neither of us was prepared for this news. On the way home from the doctor's office, we discussed how a child with Down Syndrome would change our lives. Even though we were shaken by the news, we both agreed that this child was ours to care for, regardless if his condition. We told our pastor and close family members, and began to ask God for the strength that we knew we would need.

It struck me one day that even though I never thought about Downs' babies before, God seemed to be giving me the grace to accept whatever might lie ahead. Instead of fighting the possibility, Sharon and I began preparing for it. I even found out from the parents of a Down's child that at first they were apprehensive, but later they realized what a blessing from God he was for their family. Friends and family prayed for us as we prepared to go back for the next set of tests. Sharon and I felt lifted in love to go forward in faith.

After ten long days of waiting, we had to wait another two painfully slow hours in the waiting room when our appointment was delayed. Finally, we were called into the patient room. "Do you know why you are here today?" the genetic counselor calmly asked. "Depending on the results of today's testing we want you to know what your choices are, including abortion."

The counselor's words felt like a knife in my heart. I had been preparing for a life with my son. She had just casually offered me the choice of getting rid of him. Sharon and I explained that abortion was not at all an option. We were there to gather information so we could prepare our home and our lives in the event our child had a disability. At that moment, I suddenly felt a deep sense of fatherly responsibility to begin caring for my son by fighting for his dignity and life. I realized the medical providers lacked a sense of awe for the inherent value of his existence. He was my very own flesh and blood, but he meant nothing to them. They were quite prepared to terminate his life if we gave them the word.

I asked the counselor what tests we needed to run that would ensure that we provided the best care for our child before he was born. She informed us that the first test would be a Level II Ultrasound to do a full examination of the baby in the womb. This testing confirmed we had a son. It also showed normal readings except for the long bone measurements. The nurse-specialist notified us that because of these measurements she could not rule out that he had Down Syndrome. I asked what our choices for additional testing were. Again we were advised that abortion was an option.

Our child is not a choice, I thought. *He is a baby.* It was frustrating that the medical personnel at this clinic, one of the leading teaching hospitals in the country, could not give us fundamental advice on how to help our son. Yet, no one had any difficulty giving us advice on how to terminate him. "He is not a choice for us; he is our son," I stated emphatically.

For a more certain diagnosis, we chose to have an amniocentesis done. As Sharon was being prepared for this test, our medical geneticist physician walked into the room and asked to see the series of ultrasounds that had been taken on our baby. To this day, I am not sure why he was there at that time or who sent him, but I am thankful because he stopped the amniocentesis test from being needlessly conducted. This test held the risk of possible damage to our son and a one-percent chance of miscarriage.

The latest in ultrasound equipment had arrived the day before. After completely re-running the tests himself, he found an error in the measurements taken earlier by the specialist. In the end, he confirmed that indeed my son had an abnormally large head but it was his opinion that he was just fine.

After so much waiting and negative reactions, I had trouble processing that the doctor was telling us that everything looked good. Seeing the doubt in my eyes, the doctor looked at me and quietly said "He is OK. I promise you, your son is healthy and OK." I felt weak from relief and joy. As he passed by me to leave the room, he placed a hand on my shoulder and with a smile proclaimed to the room that, "Your son is OK. However, it is my opinion that he has a large head."

When Walker was born a few months later, his eyes met mine for what seemed like an eternity. He did not cry right away, so I was worried that the doctor might have been wrong. He was not. Walker, in fact, just had a big head, like my brother and other members on my side of the family. My son and I stared at each other for a few seconds, and then he started to cry as newborns do. At that moment, I cried too—only mine were tears of joy. So many tears in fact, that I had a hard time seeing through them to cut Walker's umbilical cord.

The story of Walker's head big head did not end at birth. Our pediatrician had concerns over the size of his head through his first six months. When Walker's head size scored off their measurable comparison chart, the doctor ordered a CT scan to rule out the possibly that he had a brain tumor. There was another long wait for the test date and results. At the test, Sharon had to helplessly watch as Walker was immobilized by strapping him into a special holder to run the test. The tests were run at seven a.m. and we had to wait until almost five p.m. for the results. At the end of the day, our pediatrician finally told us, "He's OK ... He just has a big head."

That big head of Walker's is surely destined to do something great for God, although so far it has given us a lot of gray hair. But it's also given me something more. Through this experience, I learned how easily I could have lost my son. My healthy, beautiful gift from God could have so easily been discarded. Through Walker, I experienced my fatherly role as protector even before he was born.

—Sandy Blunt

Sandy Blunt is the CEO and executive director of Workforce Safety & Insurance in Bismarck, North Dakota where he lives with his wife, Sharon, and their children Alexis, five, and Walker, three. Prior to moving North Dakota in 2004, Sandy served as the chief operating officer of the Ohio Bureau of Workers' Compensation in Columbus.

Dad's Lessons in Love

My dad popped up on the Internet recently. My sister sent me the link. I clicked to open up a photo of a World War II Canadian flight crew in front of their Lancaster bomber. My dad, who had passed away eighteen years earlier, was young and handsome, and was wearing the uniform of the Royal Canadian Air Force. He stood, short in stature, next to a tall pilot and some other young, handsome crewmates.

Soon the plane would be destroyed and all those young men would be dead … except for my dad. His shortness saved him. His stature naturally assigned him to the duty of gunner in the rear turret, which was so cramped he didn't wear his parachute. Instead, he slung it on a hook. On their first mission over Germany, the plane was struck by gunfire. Dad tried to reach his mates on the radio but received no answer. He turned the platform his gun was mounted on, grabbed his chute, kicked open the hatch, and jumped. Because his chute wasn't on properly, it didn't open all the way. At about 1,000 feet before he hit the ground, the parachute bloomed and he landed safely, escaping with only minor injuries.

The photo on the Internet was posted by the niece of one of those other young men. She wanted to honor the memory of her fallen uncle. After the war, many of the relatives of the deceased crew had written to my father to find out if he knew for certain their loved ones were lost. And he wrote them all back. He had seen the bodies. There was no doubt.

After the war, my dad came home to California. He had joined the Canadian Air Force because he was born in

Canada and was still a Canadian citizen during World War II, but he grew up and lived in California. Back home, he married and had four kids. He was an ordinary man and an extraordinary father. On paper though, it might seem my dad came up short in the fatherhood department. There were times we feared the repo man. He didn't attend our school functions. He argued loudly with Mom. He stayed too long at the bar on Christmas Eve. I thought all kids waited for their dads to come home from the bar before opening presents. We all had the phone number of his favorite tavern memorized and didn't hesitate to call him to come home throughout our childhood. And he never went to Mass with us except on Easter. I loved Easter.

But he was a great father because there was never one second that we didn't know he loved our Mom and us kids to the depths of his soul.

He used to make breakfast for us every school day morning; it was always toast and eggs. Mom did pancakes on Saturdays. He was always cheerful in the morning, and we always liked our eggs "sunny side up and juicy." He often made our lunch sandwiches, too. He may have cooked so much because Mom was sick. She suffered from multiple sclerosis.

I often felt a bit deprived because we were too poor for weeklong family vacations like the ones some of my friends enjoyed. But Dad was always packing us up for day trips to the mountains or to go clamming at the beach. Mom would wake us up at four a.m. and Dad would already be in the kitchen cheerfully cooking up breakfast.

Cheerfulness. Perhaps that best describes him. And that cheerfulness is somehow the manner in which he communicated his love. Oh, he could get angry. His eyes would bulge and his voice went hoarse. We knew we had better watch out then. But mostly with us kids, he just seemed happy. And he enjoyed teasing us. He was a relentless teaser. And I don't remember his teasing ever being cruel. Not once.

When I was fourteen, my mother became an invalid. At the same time, she was very emotional and cried all the time. I was having a difficult time dealing with her suffering. I can remember crying and begging my father to put her in a rest home. He just looked at me and said, "Is that what you really want?" His strength pulled me through.

We did not put her in a nursing home. Shortly afterward, she somehow surrendered to her fate and her outbursts stopped. She, too, became cheerful.

My dad took care of his sick wife, his business, and us kids. Of course, we all pitched in. The kids took care of running the household. We had a caretaker for Mom on school days.

When I turned sixteen and could drive, I took over the grocery shopping. My sister and I took turns making the evening meals. But Dad was the champ at taking care of Mom. He still liked the bars, but he would be home if we kids couldn't be there. He took care of all Mom's personal hygiene and even changed her catheter. He was an example of selfless giving and love to us all.

I was old enough and I was a girl, so I could have been the one to care for mom. But he just asked me to help him. He never complained.

Dad wasn't a "good" Catholic in the classic sense. But he lived the Catholic life. I strive today to be like him. Shortly, before he died he told me about someone who was trying to get him to become "born again." We had never discussed theology but he explained to me, "I'm a Catholic and I'll always be a Catholic."

Later, when he was suffering at the end of his last illness, I was exhausted and frustrated. Nothing I did was right and he let me know. But at one point, I was sitting and looking at him. He was hooked up to an oxygen tank, sitting in a chair, looking at the floor. He looked up and we exchanged glances. He smiled at me. That smile reached to the depths of my soul and heart. It was his last one.

Shortly after Dad passed away, I was visiting his gravesite. It happened to be Ascension Thursday. I was worried about his salvation. I cried to God to give me a sign that Dad was OK. I went home and noticed the past Sunday's bulletin, which I hadn't read yet. I saw my father's name. Someone had the Ascension Thursday Mass celebrated for my Dad. Thanks, Lord.

Today, it is strange to look at the picture of him—on the Internet of all places—and his doomed companions. Why did God spare my father? If he had not lived, I would not have been born, nor my brothers and sisters, nor my children. I suppose that all of us living are survivors. We are survivors of the close calls of all of our ancestors. There must be a reason we made it. Our task is to find it and live it. I trust that my father did. He may not have done it perfectly, but he did it in a profound way. His life taught me what real love is all about.

—Katherine Andes

Katherine Andes is an award-winning author who writes regularly for Catholic publications. She lives in Hanford, California, and is the mother of two great kids.

Love Revealed Through the Cross

On occasion, I have had the chance to feel the love of God the Father through my own fatherhood. The one that stands out foremost in my mind was a period in my life when I was experiencing extreme pain in my arm due to a damaged vertebrae in my neck. I had not been able to sleep for weeks due to the unbearable pain constantly throbbing down my left arm. As many Catholics hear growing up, the advice to "offer up" your pain for others echoed in my mind, but I could not wrap my brain around that concept. What good could my pain possibly do?

Late one night, while all the house was asleep, I was in the living room, pacing about holding my arm and wondering how long I could last in this condition. I slumped to my knees by the couch and cried out, "God, what do you want me to do? How can you use this pain? How do I offer it up?"

All I could think of was how much suffering Jesus had gone through for my sake and for the sins of the world. I knew somehow I had to make the connection between my pain and that of the suffering Christ. For years Colossians 1:24-25 had stumped me. It says, "Now I rejoice in my sufferings for your sake, and in my flesh I complete what is lacking in Christ's afflictions for the sake of his body, that is, the church, of which I became a minister according to the divine office which was given to me for you, to make the word of God fully known." I stood up with pain-induced tears dripping from my eyes and crept up the stairs to the bedroom of one of my daughters. I knew she was struggling herself with some issues, and as her father, I could offer up my pain for her good. I knew in my head that Christ in His suffering had left me an example and that I should follow in His steps (1 Peter 2:21).

In that darkened room on my knees again, I was overcome with a joy that I had never known before. I consciously offered up my suffering in union with Christ for my child. It was at that moment that I had a deep sense of what it means to participate in Christ's suffering along with a new appreciation of how much He loved me as a son. I knew experientially that my suffering was not wasted but was actually transformed and productive in God's kingdom.

—Jeff Cavins

Jeff Cavins is the co-creator and an editor of the Amazing Grace *series. His biography appears at the end of the book.*

A Short History of Father's Day

Listening to a Mother's Day sermon in church one Sunday in May of 1909, Sonora Dodd felt the loss of her mother, who had died in childbirth delivering her sixth child. The baby survived, but Sonora's father was left a widower.

During the sermon, Sonora thought of her loving father, William Smart, a Civil War veteran who had raised all six of his children alone on a farm in the state of Washington. As an adult, Sonora understood the heroic virtue of the selfless love shown by her single father. Yet, there was no special day to honor him. Since her father was born in June, Sonora chose a Sunday in that month to hold the first Father's Day celebration in Spokane, Washington, on June 19, 1910.

At about the same time, Harry C. Meek, president of the Lions Club in Chicago, gave speeches throughout the country encouraging the establishment of a day to honor fathers. The idea caught on, and a National Father's Day committee was formed in New York City in 1926. Still, it was not until 1956 that Congress passed a joint resolution officially recognizing Father's Day.

Then, in 1966, President Lyndon B. Johnson signed a proclamation declaring that the third Sunday of June would be known as Father's Day. It was established as a permanent national observance by President Richard Nixon in 1972, nearly sixty years after Mother's Day had been proclaimed a national holiday.

Daddy's Little Girl

I remember being little enough that my father would dance with me while singing a popular tune of that era, called "Daddy's Little Girl." I would stand on the top of his shoes as we glided around the living room floor as if we were in a grand ballroom.

How I loved to dance with my father and pretend I was the belle of the ball. But suddenly, one day I could no longer dance. One early April morning in 1955, I awoke to raging fever, pain, and muscle contractions. My father scooped me up into his arms and rushed me into town to our little hospital. The diagnosis was one that struck fear into the hearts of every parent and child during that time. Polio had come to our little ballroom, and life would never be quite the same.

As we lived far from a major city, our little hospital was ill-equipped to deal with polio patients. I rapidly began to decline. Although I was supposedly unconscious, I can remember hearing the doctor speaking to my parents and telling them I would not live through the night. At that moment, my little eight-year-old mind began to pray the Angel Guardian Prayer: *There are four corners on my bed, there are four angels round my head. Now I lay me down to sleep, I pray the angels my soul to keep. If I should die before I wake, I pray the Lord my soul to take.* Suddenly, there in that dismal hospital room, angels surrounded me. I remember their beauty and how my guardian angel reached down and touched me, and told me I would be fine again one day. My life would be changed, but I would not die from the illness that was racking my body.

The next thing I remembered was my dad, sitting beside me and singing to me hour after hour.

You are the end of the rainbow, my pot of gold,
you are Daddy's little girl to have and hold.
A precious gem is what you are;
You are Mommy's bright and shining star.

You are the spirit of Christmas, my star on the tree;
You are the Easter bunny to Mommy and me.
You are sugar, you're spice, you're everything nice,
and you are Daddy's little girl.

You are the treasure I cherish so sparkling and bright,
You were touched by the holy and beautiful light.
Like angels that sing a heavenly thing,
And you are Daddy's little girl.

"Daddy's Little Girl" became his fight song. A song to cheer me up, a song to help me make it through the night, a song from his heart that echoed to mine through all of the pain.

God's amazing grace came with that beautiful song. One day, I began to recover from the worst of the illness and was sent home, crippled but alive. We could not afford big city hospitals and so our little home was quarantined. Through it all, my father never left my side. Hour after hour, day after day, my dad was beside me. He read everything he could find about polio and treatments that might strengthen my ravaged legs. From our small town library, dad found a book that was to change the course of my life. It was the autobiography of Sister Elizabeth Kenny, entitled *And They Shall Walk*.

Dad contacted the Sister Kenny Institute to learn how to do the therapy, and he doggedly began using her methods to bring my legs back to life. The therapy consisted of stretching exercises and hot packs, which burned like fire. I can still remember his big strong hands working with those hot packs. His gentle hands were red from the heat. As I would cry out in pain, Dad would cry with me and promise me it would be better. All the while he sang our battle song to keep me strong and see me through the pain.

When I could not stand the pain of having even light covers touching my body, daddy build a special cage out of chicken wire that formed a frame around my bed. This way, I could stay warm but the blankets did not touch me and cause more pain. Dad slept on the floor beside me and never let his tiredness or worries be seen. His ever-present laughter and faith in God were our constant companions throughout that terrible summer. Finally, his effort began to make a difference. Slowly but surely I could once again stand. Now we started up our little ballroom dance with earnest. Balancing me on the top of his feet, he taught me to walk once again, just as he had taught me how to dance. And of course the song was always the same ... "Daddy's Little Girl," which he sang with relish and joy each step that we took together. And the day that I stood and walked into his arms unaided, well ... I know that song was in both of our hearts.

By the time school rolled around again, I was able to walk and to return to a normal life. My dancing legs would never be quite the same, but for the most part all the muscles had come back with just minor weakness in one leg. Polio is still a part of my life, since I later developed post polio sequelae, but I will keep on dancing and remembering my father's strength and faith that God will never let us dance alone ... if we trust Him to see us through. My father will always be my favorite dance partner in my book of memories.

—Christine Trollinger

Christine Trollinger is a freelance writer from Kansas City, Missouri, whose stories have been published in several Christian books of short stories, as well as in Catholic magazines. A number of her stories have been published in two previous books in the Amazing Grace *series,* Amazing Grace for the Catholic Heart *and* Amazing Grace for Mothers. *She has three children, three grandchildren, and is great-grandmother to 2½-year-old Tyra Grace, who is the apple of her eye.*

A Perfect Gift

There's nothing like being young and in love. But when I announced my plans to get married, there was no shortage of warnings. They said, "You are too young to get married" and "Marriage is a big responsibility," along with the frequent suggestion, "Why don't you wait a few years?"

We were both eighteen and determined to prove everyone wrong. Love is all you need, right? That's what I thought anyway. A month after we exchanged vows, my wife announced she was pregnant. I had no idea that real responsibility could hit us so hard or so fast. We were both working and attending college on top of it all.

I was nineteen in 1961 when the words, "It's a boy!" were announced to me. What a thrill to have a son of my own. But work and school demanded my attention. So did my wife and son. I felt there was not enough time for it all, so I focused on school and work, neglecting my family. Four months into fatherhood, I found myself alone. My wife had left with my son.

My promises to do better fell on deaf ears. My fatherhood was done mostly absentee with mere visits. When my son, Russ, was eight months old, his mother asked if I would take him "for the weekend." I gladly accepted.

That "weekend" turned out to be a long one. It would be twenty-six years before Russ laid eyes on his mother again, with one minor exception. She showed up suddenly when Russ was twelve months old and threatened to take him away from me. My son no longer even recognized his mother. She was a complete stranger to him by that point. But this was the 60s, a time when men rarely got custody. I lost a lot of sleep worrying, but by the time Russ was eighteen months old, I was granted full custody in the divorce. Despite my youth, I had become a father through and through.

Initially, I lived with my parents, but by the end of the first year I was on my own. I was daddy, chief cook, bottle washer, student, and sole bread winner. Unable to afford disposables, I even washed cloth diapers. As much as I loved my son, my role as a single parent was exhausting. Fortunately, I worked with two other men who were also single dads. It helped knowing I was not the only single father on the planet. Still, I often felt abandoned, lonely, and like a huge failure. I managed to get a good job and advanced to a surprisingly high level, but the college degree I had sought had to be sacrificed. There just was not enough time in the day.

There was plenty of time, however, to feel resentment toward my ex-wife. I imagined her enjoying a carefree lifestyle at my expense. While I washed diapers and dishes, she was probably going out to dinner, dancing, and laughing with her single friends.

Eventually I met and married a woman who had an 18-month-old little girl named Hannah. Russ now had a mother and a sister. We were no longer just a bachelor father and his son; we felt like a real family. Russ grew tall and strong, and became a darn good kid under our care.

One weekend, shortly before Russ had left home, he had helped me build and install a great redwood hot tub. While soaking in it one evening, I thought about him just finishing boot camp at the age of eighteen and being assigned to an aircraft carrier, the USS Constellation. I was so proud of him. Alone with my thoughts in the stillness of the early morning, I missed my son.

At that very moment, in a flash, bitterness I had felt toward his mother for so many years washed away. The part of me that had nursed the grudge for so long filled in with gratitude. For the first time, insight revealed what a gift she had given me. Nothing in the world could ever match such a gift. My Russ! Of course, I had loved him from the start, but I always harbored resentment that she had abandoned us. Now, I realized that my resentment had blinded me for too long. I was not a victim; I was blessed. Russ's mother had carried him for nine long months and brought him into the world through her pain and effort. While she unfortunately missed out on all that joy and love, I did not. She had given me my son, the greatest gift of all.

—Raf Leon Dahlquist

Russ is now forty-five, and Hannah is forty-one. Raf has four grandchildren ranging from five to twenty-five. Despite never receiving a college degree, Raf has fourteen patents and has traveled world-wide as an invited lecturer on the subject of inductively coupled plasma atomic emission spectroscopy.

Lessons From Papa

Standing outside the pillars of St. Peter's Square stood a dentist from Minnesota. That dentist was my father and a man of wisdom and faith. A warm, fatherly grin rested comfortably upon his sunburned face. His complexion appeared redder next to his bright white hair beneath his white baseball cap. Traveling with my mother and me, he waited in anticipation for the audience of another white-haired, wise old man, Pope Benedict XVI. This trip to Rome was a college graduation gift to me from my parents.

As the barricades outside St. Peter's Square were removed, pilgrims pushed and shoved their way toward the entrances, all filled with great fervor for the Holy Father. Handing my backpack to my father, I planned to squeeze my way through the massive crowd and save seats at the papal audience for my parents. Dodging short, pointy-elbowed nuns and elderly Italian women, I approached the closest entrance only to be thwarted by Murphy's Law. As I was about to pass through the police-guarded metal detector, the machine broke down. Panic stricken, I headed to another point of entry. I was swallowed up by the mob and the intensity of the morning rush fueled my excitement for the day. Eager to see the Vicar of Christ, yet frustrated by the ardent crowds, I begged the pardon of those around as I squeezed back to the front of the line. After much delay, I was inside the pillars of St. Peter's Square.

My father entered the Square at the same time as I did, holding both of our bags. Our meeting was unexpected but timely. Pops was our pack mule, and it was expected for him to be the last one to reach our seats. With the advantage of being thirty-four years younger than he, I took the heaviest bag from my father and sprinted toward the main stage's innermost point of entry. There were more barricades set up for funneling the mad rush of visitors to their seats. For a moment, the mob resembled a herd of sheep rushing to the shepherd. Not finding an entry point into the barricades, Pops and I opted for our own means of admission. I was skinny enough to squeeze through the barricade and into the funnel, and like the track star he never was, my dad hurdled the obstruction to join me.

Leaving my father behind, I sprinted for the steps of St. Peter's Basilica. My heart pounding and my brow sweating, I gave the great race a final push to the finish line. With my eyes on the prize, I had made it to the special reserved seats near the chair of the Holy Father. To my bewilderment, my mother was already waiting for us at our seats. She was standing next to a priest friend and traveling companion of ours, who had attended many papal audiences and knew exactly where to go. Mom had stayed with him like his shadow. Without missing a beat, she poked fun at my surprised reaction. Huffing and puffing, my father the hurdler joined us at our seats.

With our Minnesotan hearts still racing from the run and the excitement of the day, we basked in the Roman sun awaiting the Holy Father's arrival. We began to cheer as Pope Benedict XVI rode out to the Square in the back of the pope-mobile. Speaking in many languages, the Holy Father addressed the multitude, and then gave his benediction. The hand of the Pope directed me to my father as he moved his hand down in the familiar cross-shaped pattern. On the downward motion of the cross, the Holy Father's hand seemed to stall in three places: pointing towards heaven, resting in front of him, and pointing down to the faithful.

His act seemed to suggest the following narration: "Be blessed from the love of God the Father. Be guided by the direction of the Holy Father, and live by the example of your earthly father." The Vicar of Christ, the man I had traveled thousands of miles to see, used the physical motion of the benediction to spiritually lead me back to my father, my first teacher of the faith.

After the audience, His Holiness once again rode in the back of his custom ride. The vehicle drove slowly through the crowd to allow the Holy Father to shake hands and kiss babies. Crowding close to the barricade, I stood atop my chair—towering above the horde and placing myself at eye level with Pope Benedict XVI. The pope-mobile stopped directly in front of me, and the Holy Father reached out for a baby to kiss on the head. The Pope's white hair beneath the white zucchetto resembled another white-haired, white-capped man I know who loves the faith and his family. After returning the baby, His Holiness, though facing me, looked both at me and beyond me. With a soft, fatherly expression on his face, he seemed to invite me to turn my attention not to him, but to the father who had spent a lifetime calling me to be the man I am becoming. Upon this recognition, Pope Benedict XVI and I locked eyes. The gaze filled me with a sense of awe and wonder. It was his eyes that begged me to remain faithful, just as my father was faithful. I reached out my hand, and with the extra push from my mother and the support of my father beneath me, I held the hand of the Vicar of Christ. His grip was like his pontificate: firm and gentle. As he passed by, my eyes turned to my father, on whom I had been leaning.

I had desired so greatly to meet the Holy Father, a man of great importance to me. Hoping that our meeting would cultivate a deeper devotion to my faith, His Holiness did not leave me disappointed. The good and gentle Shepherd provoked a moment of wonder and thanks in me for the one who laid the foundation of my faith: my own father.

—Zachary Bennett

Zachary Bennett's biography appears after "The Good Race Run Together," found earlier in this chapter.

A Father's Interpretation of I Corinthians 13

If I manage a staff of many but have not managed my family, I have managed nothing.

And if I negotiate the deal of deals while neglecting my children, I have negated the opportunity of a lifetime—in fact, my God–appointed duty as father.

If I become a head of state but fail to assume my role as head of the household, I am but unemployed.

And if I consult executives, yet have not been available to my own children for consultation, I remain the misguided one.

If I prioritize my workday/career but do not prioritize my home life, I have prioritized a progressive distancing of those who mean the most to me.

If I earn great wealth and respect among my peers through business accomplishment, yet I fail to earn the respect of my wife and children, I am reduced to a very poor man.

If I travel the world pursuing my goals, yet am not available to drive my son to his ballgame or my daughter to her recital, I have indeed boarded the wrong plane.

And if I bestow all my accomplishment to provide for my family, and if I work until utter exhaustion, but do not make time with my family a priority, it profits me nothing.

And yes, I must keep in perspective that if a man won't work, neither shall he eat, and if a man won't provide for his family he is worse than an infidel.

Should I choose, however, to tolerate the devastating demands society has placed on family values, God help me, for I have failed to recognize that toleration is the first stop to deterioration.

Time can never be recaptured once it is passed. Time will not even pause for a moment. Nor will time be forgiving as it is fleeing away.

Time spent together cannot be measured, for those precious moments become priceless memories to the beholder.

When I was a child, I thought like a child, cherishing each moment together when I took my daddy's hand. When I became a father, I recaptured that moment each time my little girl took her daddy's hand.

For now those memories seem as fresh as yesterday. And had I known then what I have not learned until now, I would have spent just an extra minute at home instead of at the office.

And now abide Time Management, Quality Time, Quantity Time, these three; but the greatest of these is Time itself spent with your children!

—John G. "Giovanni" Grippando

In addition to being a proud father, John G. "Giovanni" Grippando is a member of Who's Who Worldwide (Registry of Global Business Leaders), an Entrepreneur of the Year nominee, and a Mr. Future Business Executive recipient. He has worked as a senior management consultant, speaks several languages, and enjoys writing poetry. His work has appeared in the Chicken Soup *series of books. He can be contacted at JohnGiovanni@Juno.com*

Father to Many

My father loved being "Dad" to his seven children. Kids seem to absorb such examples, so fatherhood found a natural resting place in my heart. Yet, early on in my life, I felt called to a different sort of fatherhood—the priesthood. *I will be a father to a parish family,* I thought. I also felt called to be with the "least of my brothers" and loved building things with my hands. So, as a young carpenter, I joined the Glenmary Home Missioners as a brother, building homes for the poor in Appalachia. My goal was eventually to become a priest.

Then, in 1981, at Catholic University of America in Washington, D.C., I met Donna. She had spent a summer caring for street children in India for Mother Teresa. She, too, had felt drawn to be merciful to the least among us and had even considered joining a community of sisters. With our love of God and desire to serve Him as our common ground, we fell in love. Though love bloomed quickly, we proceeded cautiously and sought God's guidance to be certain that marriage was the vocation to which we were being called. Three years after our first meeting, we married.

Donna took a job teaching in Philadelphia and I started a contracting business renovating houses. With a stable marriage, good jobs, and a healthy savings, we looked forward to starting a family. Donna and I were ready for God to send us as many children as He wanted us to have. We hoped there would be many.

But month after month we failed to conceive. Something was wrong. We were devastated. Over the course of many months we went to several different doctors and fertility experts. As we progressed with diagnosis and treatment we eventually reached an impassable bridge. Doctors counseled us to try in-vitro fertilization. This treatment, though, is contrary to the teachings of the Church because it separates the act of love between husband and wife with procreation. There would have to be some other way for us to become parents.

Before we had gotten married, both of us had a heart for abandoned children. We knew such children could slip easily into our lives. Although we still prayed for Donna to get pregnant, we also visited a non-profit adoption agency. Donna found the photograph of a one-year-old girl in Mexico named Rosa in a book of orphans waiting to be placed for adoption. We knew instantly in our hearts that she was meant for us. "That's our first child, I just know it," Donna told me.

But the officials at the orphanage were not as enthusiastic. Rosa was scheduled for open-heart surgery. They encouraged us to select another child instead of waiting for her. "No," we told the officials in Mexico, "We will pray for Rosa's surgery and we will wait."

Eight months later we flew down to Mexico and returned with Rosa. Because of Rosa's special needs, Donna quit her teaching job to stay home full-time. I continued my contracting business, but I looked forward to coming home each night to see my beloved daughter.

While we continued to pray for Donna to get pregnant, God continued to direct us to more children with special needs in orphanages in other countries. Each night Donna and I prayed that God would bring us children that needed us. We wanted more children like Rosa, the poor orphan girl no one wanted.

Two years later, Natalie joined our family. As an infant, she had been brought to an orphanage in Guatemala by her mother, who was unable to care for her. It was a joy to add one more to our little family. Shortly after adopting Natalie, Donna was in church praying. She was suddenly overcome with the feeling that God's plan for our lives was to care for abandoned children—as many as we could handle. When Donna shared her feeling with me, it was if she was telling me something I already knew. Yes, God was directing us to something big. The problem was money. We had used up our savings on the first two adoptions. Yet, we knew that if taking in more children was God's plan for us, He would take care of the details.

Our next step was to become foster parents with the state of Pennsylvania. It was a way for us to care for children without coming up with the money to cover the expenses ourselves. Our first foster child became our first son, David. His mother had been pressured to have an abortion but resisted. She was too emotionally unstable to raise him herself. We found him to be such a blessing.

Our next child, Maria Elena, came to us through our daughter Rosa, who was seven at that time. Twelve-year-old Maria Elena was visiting the United States on a summer sponsorship program. The two girls met on an outing and discovered they were from the same orphanage. Rosa immediately felt a deep bond with this girl. She turned to Donna and said: "Mom, I think God wants that girl to be my big sister." We felt it, too. But there was no money. Still we had to try and to trust. A yard sale and donations from the church and community brought us the $12,000 we needed to adopt Maria Elena.

Over the years, one by one, the orphanage in Mexico, social service workers, and others contacted us and asked if we had room for "one more." They were babies and young children for the most part with some sort of handicaps, physical challenges, emotional issues, or a combination of all three. Whenever we were asked to take in another, Donna and I felt it was God asking. So how could we say no?

We knew a traditional school would not work with Mary Elena's language barrier, so we began home schooling our children as we continued to add more. We took in a biracial foster baby, Peter, taken from his parents due to neglect. Shortly thereafter, we accepted Dominic, who had been born to a crack-addicted mother. But at this point, we thought we had to surrender to our human limitations. Peter cried a frequent mournful cry and refused to let us get close to him. As much as we loved him, he would not let us in. We came to believe that Peter needed to be in a family without other children so he could get more attention than we could give. He was placed in just such a home. We wanted what was best for Peter, but his absence left a hole in our heart. We accepted it as the will of God and continued to pray that God would allow us to help other children.

Within four months, we adopted eleven-year-old Sandra from Mexico. Also, at this time, we received a call from a medical center's burn unit. Peter had been severely burned. I had loved Peter as my own son and had struggled when we gave him up, thinking it was in his best interests. Donna and I would never again let him go.

Through Peter, we began learning about reactive attachment disorder and realized there were signs of the syndrome in some of our other children. Given their early loss and in some cases neglect and abuse, establishing a relationship—even with loving parents—was difficult for them. They had put up walls and even seemed to reject us at times. We learned that our kids needed our unconditional love and needed us to be there for them, even during their bad times. My children taught me the true meaning of a father's unconditional love. Even though they seemed to reject it at times—just as we at times reject our Heavenly Father's love—through the grace of God, I was able to keep loving them.

The ink on Peter's adoption papers had barely dried when Dominic's biological mother called us from prison. She was pregnant and wanted her baby to be with his brother. Of course we said yes. Later on, we would be present in the delivery room at the birth of the third brother, Joseph. We kept adding until we had reached eleven children. Any large family would be time consuming, but we had children with special needs. Even though I could take some of the older children with me to work and often came home when there was a crisis, I realized that my work as a contractor was interfering with the demands of my family. They needed a full-time father. *But how can I provide an income for our family and stay home full-time?* I wondered. Donna and I prayed. We both felt I needed to be home. *But is this feeling from God?* we wondered. We placed our trust in our Heavenly Father and trusted that if this was His will, He would provide.

We sold our house in Havertown, Pennsylvania, and became incorporated as Saint Joseph's House. We knew there could be no better patron for our home than St. Joseph, the foster father of Jesus. He protected us and guided us throughout this risky endeavor. Initially, a priest offered an abandoned convent in the inner city for us to live in until we could find a more suitable place, as this not an ideal situation for our children. And then one day, after our story was told in a national publication, we received many generous donations, including a large home in East Fallowfield, Pennsylvania.

As of this writing, we have nineteen children, all of whom we home school. This would not be possible without the generosity of many people, both locally and throughout the world.

Through the grace of God, I am the father of children no one else wanted. I would not trade places with anyone. We bring our children to Jesus one soul at a time. Our lives are about teaching them about being faithful and forgiving. We go to daily Mass, pray the Rosary, and attend Eucharistic adoration. We have a wonderful priest who comes to our home to hear confessions and a Carmelite community nearby that gives us spiritual nourishment.

What I have learned from these wonderful children that have made me a father is that none of us is perfect; we all make it to the Kingdom limping along. Donna and I are gathering up these children for God and leading them to be perfected in the kingdom to come.

Each night Donna and I prayed for adopted and biological children. Essentially we prayed—and still do— that the Lord's will be done. Children who need a family like ours, we trust He will send them here. We also continue to pray for biological children as well. Hope springs eternal.

—John Kurtz

John and Donna Kurtz are incorporated as Saint Joseph's House with the goal of advancing the teachings of Jesus Christ and His Church and promoting a respect for life in all its stages across all levels of society. They can be contacted by email jkurtz@saintjosephhouse.com

Chapter 2
A Father's Strength

Our Last Meal

I gazed out the window into a dreary Wednesday morning. The steady stream of rain was fitting, as if even the sky were crying for my father. "Is he still alive?" I sighed, wondering if Dad had made it through the night. "He must have, I decided, or surely someone from the hospital would have called to let me know."

It would seem to be a big leap from a mere broken arm to the threshold of death, but for my elderly father it had been but a quick, small step. Dad had lived alone on the farm since December of 2000, when my mother—suffering from Alzheimer's—had entered a nursing home. Seven weeks later, on St. Valentine's Day, Mom died from a blood clot in her lungs.

Dad was lonely without his wife of nearly fifty-two years, but he remained relatively active. Then, in June of 2003, he fell and and broke his right arm. Given that he was eighty and because of the type of break, the orthopedic surgeon advised against surgery. His arm healed of its own accord, but it was never again useful to Dad. Maybe it was losing use of his arm, or maybe he was tired of living alone, or perhaps it was just plain old age; whatever it was, Dad began a noticable decline.

In late May of the following year, Dad fell on the floor between the kitchen and the back porch resulting in him breaking his left arm—his good one. He was taken to the Minneapolis VA Medical Center.

"Hi, Dad," I greeted him in his hospital room. "How are you doing?"

"I'm so confused," Dad cried. "I don't know why I'm here."

"Oh, Dad, you fell and broke your good arm," I explained.

"Oh, oh, oh," he cried. I could see the hurt in his eyes. He knew what that meant. There was no way he could go back home alone now. I knew from a previous conversation we had that he never wanted to leave the farm. Dad was independent and did not want to be a burden on anyone. I remembered his comment to me years earlier about living in a nursing home. "I'd rather take a bullet than live in one of those places," he had said. But for now, there was no point in upsetting him and talking about the future.

A Eucharistic minister stopped by and offered Holy Communion to Dad. Although he had never been overtly religious, Dad had always kept God in his life. He readily accepted Communion. It made it easier for me to leave him that day. At least I knew he was not alone. He had Jesus.

"I'll be back tomorrow," I promised. Driving home, my mind became flooded with the busy week ahead. I wanted to be present for my dad in his time of need, like he had been there for my four siblings and me so many times when we were growing up. I would just have to do my best, I determined. My two brothers and sisters would be visiting, too. One sister, Chris, lived in Des Moines, Iowa. I prayed for God to help my Dad and for the ability to be a good daughter.

On Tuesday, Dad had suffered respiratory arrest and had to be put on a ventilator. It was time to call Chris home.

On Wednesday, we all gathered in Dad's hospital room. Even though he had been administered morphine to ease his pain, Dad recognized us all. We were all grateful that he was still able to visit with us. On Saturday, it became apparent that Dad would likely need a feeding tube soon. Yet, he was still cognizant enough to understand the plan. He shook his head "no" when we brought up the feeding tube. Dad made it clear he did not want it. "What about the ventilator?" my sister asked, knowing he needed it to keep breathing. Again he shook his head "no." He was informed that his breathing would be difficult without it. Still, he shook his head. His decision was made.

Dad kept hanging on and we, his children, took turns at his side. On Sunday, we all gathered together when his ventilator was removed, a decision allowed by the Church. He was awake and asked again if he was sure he wanted it out. He was. "Good girl," he whispered to my sister, who was standing at his side.

For the next two days, my siblings and I took shifts at the hospital. I had spent so much time at Dad's side that I did not worry that he might pass while I was away. On Wednesday morning, I looked out into the rain and wondered if he was still alive. Since no one had called, I headed out to the hospital again.

Entering the room, Dad's breath was labored but regular. I took his hand in mine and cried. My once strong father was suffering so; struggling with each breath. "What are you waiting for?" I cried softly. As much as I would miss him, I wanted his pain to be over.

My sister, Chris, entered the room and together we spoke gently and lovingly to our father. We both wondered what Dad was waiting for. "Maybe there's someone he's still waiting for or maybe there's someone we still need to meet,"

Chris surmised. We went to lunch and returned to Dad's room, believing it would not be much longer.

At 2:45, a loud rap at the hospital door startled us. "Come in," we both chimed. A tall, dark-haired man in his 30s stepped into the room. He had glasses, a beard, and mustache, and a large crucifix hung from his neck. Holding his clipboard, he asked, "Is this George Robinson?"

We quickly glanced at one another and cautiously answered in the affirmative. "Well, I'd like to give him Holy Communion," the tall man informed us. Again, Chris and I looked at one another.

"But he's in a coma now," Chris explained.

The man smiled gently, "I will give him only a very small piece."

"I don't know..." Chris hesitated.

"Only a particle," he assured us.

Finally, we agreed that it would be a good thing for Dad to receive one last Holy Communion. The man broke off a very small piece for Dad. I received the remaining host. My sister then received also.

"This is probably the last meal he will have before he dies," I commented to the man.

"Isn't it cool that you got to share his last meal with him?" the man said. Then he said promised to pray for Dad and left.

A calm came over Chris and me. It really was "cool" to have shared Dad's last meal with him. We held his hands. His breathing became lighter and easier. Then, suddenly, he slipped away. It was 3:23. Chris and I looked at each other in awe. His struggle was over and it had been so peaceful. I told the nurse, who sent for the hospital chaplain. He arrived with a chaplain-in-training at his side.

"Is there anything I can do for you?" he asked.

"He just received Holy Communion and quietly slipped away," Chris explained. "I don't think we need anything else now."

The chaplain looked startled. "Who was it? Who gave him Communion?"

I described the man and the chaplain looked even more perplexed. "There was no one scheduled to distribute Communion today," he said. He again expressed his sympathy and left the room looking very confused.

We stayed a while longer, so say our final good-byes to Dad. Before we left the hospital, we stopped by the nurses' station. We had grown close to the nurse on duty and she had asked us to come say good-bye before we left. When we told her about Dad receiving Communion, she, too, became perplexed. "I didn't see anyone distributing Communion on this floor today," she said.

Chris and I went to dinner together that evening to process Dad's passing. "Who was that man?" we both wondered. Then, we recalled Chris's statement about Dad still waiting for someone before he let go. We were waiting for this man who appeared in the room and Dad was waiting for Jesus. I was so sad when I arrived at the hospital that day, just as the disciples on the road to Emmaus were sad. Then, just as his disciples recognized Him, I recognized Jesus in the breaking of the bread and my sadness disappeared. "Who was that man?" we wondered again. "An angel? Jesus Himself?"

The reading we chose for Dad's funeral had to be the story of the disciples on the road to Emmaus. Jesus had been with us on the last walk together with Dad. We may have parted ways with him on this earth, but we are forever united with him in Christ.

—Katie Alfveby

Katie Alfveby lives in Elk River, Minnesota, and has been married to Dave for seventeen years. They have three boys: Ben, fourteen, Dan, eleven, and Joel, seven. They are involved in both the church the school. Katie loves to read and is one of two "story tellers" at the Elk River Public Library.

Like Father, Like Daughter

"Daddy, please!" I pleaded with my father.

"No," he insisted. "It's not going to happen." Then, to signify the conversation was over, he walked out of the room.

My daddy, Horval Jones, could be as stubborn as the mules he owned. The problem was that in this case, his stubborn streak could cost him his life.

Daddy was suffering from an incurable kidney disease called glomerulonephritis. In the fall of 1998, he had begun to appear very fatigued. Growing up, I always looked up to my father as invincible. He owned a logging business in Mississippi and always had energy to spare. But suddenly, it seemed like he had little strength for much of anything. Whenever I asked him if he was OK, Daddy brushed my questions aside and changed the subject.

It was finally my mother who revealed the truth to me. "He doesn't want anyone to know," she confided in me. "In a few years, his kidneys will completely shut down." My mother explained that Daddy did not want to be treated like a patient nor receive sympathy. Daddy was only fifty-seven. I could not imagine him being taken from us while he was still so young.

Two years later, his kidneys stopped functioning and his name was placed on a transplant waiting list. Three days a week of dialysis kept him alive. Yet, it was not the sort of life he had once lived. The disease robbed him of his former energy and enthusiasm. My sisters, Stacey and Kim, and I were not willing to watch him just slip away. We offered Daddy one of our kidneys. Our brother was running the logging business for him and had also recently suffered serious injuries from a car accident, so we would not let him offer a kidney. But Daddy also would not consider one of our kidneys.

"I've lived a good life," he said. "I'm not about to risk one of yours."

More months passed and Daddy grew weaker. I was frustrated by his stubborn refusal to accept our help, until it hit me. *I'm just like Daddy,* I thought. *I can be as stubborn as he is and I'm not going to take "no" for an answer.*

Without telling him, I called the hospital to find out what a person needed to do in order to become a kidney donor. I learned that first they would need to determine if I was a match. When I told my sisters about it, we all agreed to get tested. Our hope was that if one of us was a match, maybe we could get Daddy to reconsider.

A few weeks later, just days after his fifty-ninth birthday, the hospital informed us that all three sisters were a match. We prayed hard that Daddy would accept one of our kidneys. Surrounded by his daughters, Daddy broke down and gave in when we told him we were all a match and we all wanted to give him a kidney.

"I don't know what to say," he choked. Looking from face to face, our love overpowered him. "OK," he tearfully accepted.

Daddy had given so much of himself to us while we were young. He filled our childhood with trail rides and gardening and with his loving companionship. Now, we needed to decide which sister would give a part of herself back to Daddy. It was not just my stubbornness that won the day, but it seemed practical that I should be the donor. My other sisters both held jobs and one sister was still hoping for another child. I was a stay-at-home mom. My son, Cas, was seven, and Abbie was five. After two C-sections, I did not think that we would have any more children. It made the most sense that I would be the donor.

I joked to my dad, "We all decided that since I'm the prettiest and smartest, it should be me."

Daddy laughed, "Why am I not surprised?"

Then, just when we thought everything was settled, the phone rang late one night. It was my mother. "Your father's had a heart attack," she sobbed.

My heart sank. *Were we going to lose Daddy after all?* I wondered. *Please, God,* I prayed. *Don't take him from us yet.*

He slipped in and out of consciousness for the next few days. When he finally came to, we learned that his heart was only pumping at fifteen percent of normal capacity. The doctor ruled out a transplant unless his heart recovered to at least thirty percent. "Otherwise, he'll never survive," the doctor explained.

It was like a knife in my own heart watching Daddy's face fall. "Well," he shrugged. "I guess that's that."

That's when I realized my own stubborn streak must be even stronger than Daddy's. I was not ready to give up yet. "What do you mean?" I demanded. "You heard the doctor. You can have a transplant if your heart is beating at thirty percent. So get to work."

In spite of his condition, Daddy gave a weak smile. "Always the stubborn one," he whispered.

When he came home from the hospital, it was hard for him to even stand. Through prayer, I became more determined than ever that God planned for me to give one of my kidneys to Daddy. If it was God's will, I knew nothing would stand in the way. I went ahead with the tests that needed to be done prior to donating the kidney. Then, I trusted in Divine Providence.

"I'm doing my part, so you do yours," I told Daddy.

At first, he forced himself to stand, then to walk across the room, then to climb stairs. Soon he was walking to the farthest pasture. Three months later, his heart was beating at thirty-one percent. God even gave us an extra one percent to show his faithfulness.

On October 29, 2001, just before Daddy and I were wheeled into pre-op, we squeezed each other's hands. "We can do it," I said with a smile.

In the recovery room, I opened my eyes. My family was gathered around me. Mamma smiled at me and said, "They called us from the surgery, Sam. Your kidney functioned immediately."

"Thank you, God," I prayed. I never doubted for a moment that everything was going to work out.

It's been four years since the surgery. Our recoveries went very well and the new kidney gave my father a new lease on life. Then, in 2005, my husband Larry and I had another gift to share with Daddy. We gave him another grandson—our surprise baby, Luke. We thank God every day for all the new life he has put into our family.

—Samantha Winstead

Larry and Sam Winstead run their own logging business in Philadelphia, Mississippi. Sam does the bookkeeping from home in between caring for her three children, who are now eleven, nine, and one. Her father keeps busy playing with his grandchildren and growing a garden big enough for the whole family to harvest.

A Man's Man

He was one of Rochester, New York's greatest athletes in the 1950s. When I was sixteen and in my physical prime, he was in his 40s, but he beat me in the forty-yard dash like I was standing still. He could have played for anybody. The Cubs wanted to talk to him. The Yankees would have if he'd been interested.

Instead he took a job at the local tool and die to be close to his aging parents. It's a good thing, too; otherwise he never would have met my mother. Family came first.

His generation of fathers hadn't heard of "quality time," but the idea would not have impressed him. He never contented himself with just fitting his kids into his schedule when it was convenient. He knew that being there for "crummy time" is what counts: the phone call at three a.m. from a stranded child needing a ride home; the sobs of a son failing to make friends at a new school; the cries of an infant whose fever would not break.

My father and I were at daggers' ends during my teen years. It was the usual stuff: I thought I knew everything, and he thought that yelling at me would bring me to my senses. Yet, he was always there. I had my sights set on becoming a boxing champion from the age of twelve. When I was fifteen, I had a preliminary match against a much stronger fighter whom I was going to have to fight again a few days later. I lost that first match—badly. That night, Dad found me retching in the bathroom, devastated. He said, "I know tonight was rough, but you have a chance to redeem yourself this weekend. You've worked too hard. Don't you dare throw away three years like this." He gave me the courage to go back for the rematch and win. It is one of my most cherished memories of my father.

We always worried about his health due to his smoking. I once thought that a "cigarette load" might help him quit. For the uninitiated, a cigarette load is a splinter of wood caked in gunpowder that you slip into a cigarette or cigar. Once, I packed a load into his kitchen-drawer stash of smokes and forgot about it. A couple of weeks later, as I watched cartoons nearby, he stumbled into the kitchen early one Saturday morning, lit up a cigarette, and "bang!" — the load worked as promised. He shouted, "Rick! That's not funny!" and then chuckled for several minutes while lighting up another one.

After a rough day watching doctors work to revive him when his health finally failed, I said to my mother in frustration, "He treated his body like a rented mule." She responded, "That mule carried us all." And carry us he did. In the middle of the worst economic crisis since the Great Depression, he made the commitment to send his children to Catholic high schools. He supported his own father until the end. He sacrificed driving fancy cars so that his wife could stay home and raise his children. Those same children never knew what it was like to write a college tuition check.

If you are a father, the most haunting passage in all of Scripture must be at the end of the gospel of John. Our Risen Lord has just conferred primacy to Peter over the apostles by the Sea of Tiberias. Christ asks him three times, "Do you love Me?" An exasperated Peter tells Him, "You know I love you." Christ responds, "Truly, truly, I say to you, when you were young, you girded yourself and walked where you would; but when you are old, you will stretch out your hands, and another will gird you and carry you where you do not wish to go" (Jn 21:18). Love demands sacrifice. In an age that tells us to assert our own identities and to get our share, my father knew that a life lived well requires more.

—Richard Leonardi

Rich Leonardi, publisher of the blog "Ten Reasons" (richleonardi.blogspot. com), grew up in his father's house in Rochester, New York, and currently lives with his wife and five children in Cincinnati, Ohio.

Dad to the Rescue

Standing outside the kindergarten door, I scanned the room searching for the face of my son, Eric.

I often volunteer my computer expertise at my son's school, and the computer teacher had called me that morning requesting assistance. "I'll come by during my lunch hour," I promised. The problem was fixed rather quickly. As I turned down the hall to return to work, the urge came over me to peek into Eric's room.

I'll just make eye contact and wave to him, I thought. But standing outside the darkened room, I couldn't locate Eric among the sea of kids lying on mats watching a video. Several of them spotted me.

"Teacher, there's a man at the door," some of the children announced.

The teacher met me at the door and whispered, "I can't believe you are here. Eric is in the bathroom and I think he's having a problem."

I walked to the bathroom in the back of the room and gently knocked. "Eric, it's me, Dad."

When the door opened, my son's face went from panic to relief. He was indeed having a major problem. Eric apparently had not made it to the toilet in time. His five-year-old abilities were no match for the mess. He had struggled to clean things up but instead, had spread the mess everywhere.

Cleaning it up was beyond the capability of a child, so his only option would have been the humiliation of calling across the room to the teacher for help. School protocol would have required the teacher to call a parent to come and help with such a sensitive situation. One could only imagine the embarrassment such a scene would bring down on a young boy. Surely the circumstance would have meant snickers from the kids and an emotional scar for my son.

Instead, the providential happened: Dad just happened to be at the bathroom door at the exact moment when Eric probably felt he had never needed me more. The look in my son's eyes said it all—his Dad was here now, so everything would be OK. It was incredible to help my child in a time of such need. In fact, to this day I haven't experienced a more powerful fatherly moment. There seemed to be the secure notion that, of course I was there. If Eric had been older, he would have had the intellectual ability to process the extreme unlikelyhood of my happening upon him by chance at such a crucial moment.

I cleaned him up and sent him back into the classroom where the kids were too engrossed in the video to notice his return. Neither did they notice the extra time I remained in the bathroom to clean things up.

God surely must have directed me to my son that day. It seemed like such a small thing—stopping by his classroom—but it turned out to be a major save for my son. I believe coincidence was really a God-incidence. And it gave me a glimpse into the trust of a child who has faith in the care of his earthly father, just as we can trust in the care of our Heavenly Father.

—Steve Bowen

In the Paws of Aslan

Looking around the patient waiting room, I wondered how much longer it would be until the neurologist came in with the results of my MRI. Like most boys of twelve, waiting for anything seemed to slow the clock down. But with my life on the line, the hours I had been waiting were like an eternity.

Finally, the neurologist came in. His smile betrayed nothing as he ruffled my brown hair and casually asked how I was doing. Then, he called my parents in. He excused himself to speak with them privately in his office. Again, I sat alone in the cold, sterile patient room, awaiting news of my fate. *It can't be good*, I deduced, *or the doctor could have talked in front of me.*

When everyone returned, my parents' strained faces and red eyes revealed it was bad news. Gently placing his hands on my shoulders, the doctor leveled with me: "Daniel, you have a brain tumor."

He went on to explain that the egg-sized tumor was lodged in my cerebellum. It was unknown at that point whether it was malignant or had reached the brain stem. If either were the case, survival was unlikely. Regardless, surgery was necessary. Even in the best case scenario, if the tumor was non-cancerous and not on the brain stem, there was still a risk that my balance, swallowing, and speech would be affected. I thought of my active life. *Would I still be able to play soccer or jump off a diving board?* I wondered.

In the eleven days remaining before my surgery, I learned how much I meant to people. The love and concern was not surprising coming from my family and friends, but even complete strangers came forward with gifts and attention. Although I would have traded it all to go back to my regular life, it helped the days pass. Yet, at night in my bed, the approaching surgery haunted me. *Are these my last days?* I wondered. As the countdown to surgery progressed, I asked lots of questions about heaven and wanted my mom to sleep in my room with me. In spite of their pain, my parents revealed a strong faith in God's will for me. They trusted that I was in His hands.

During those eleven days I chose *The Last Battle* by C.S. Lewis for my usual nightime reading with Mom. It's the final book in the *Chronicles of Narnia* series about a fictional land protected by Aslan, a loving and powerful lion. Fierce invaders are approaching Narnia and will likely destroy it. When the battle is at hand, a child whispers her fears to the king. "Courage, child," he replies. "We are all between the paws of Aslan."

Those words sunk deep into my being. "Mom, that's where I am," I announced. "I'm safe between the hands of God." I knew that in spite of my fear, God was holding me and I could trust Him.

The pre-dawn drive to the hospital was quiet. My parents prayed with me, hugged me, and expressed their trust that God was with me. When I opened my eyes in the intensive care unit after the eight-hour surgery, I immediately closed them again. My head throbbed with pain greater than I had ever imagined. The slightest movement caused the six-inch incision in the back of my skull to radiate a pounding agony. On top of that, I was vomiting every few minutes. I could not even keep down the regular strength Tylenol—the strongest pain killer I was allowed.

My dad sat quitely at my side. When he saw I needed to vomit, he gently held my head as still as possible and then slipped it back on my pillow. Sleep was out of the question. I might doze off for a minute or two, only to wake up to throw up again. I could barely even cry out because it only magnified the pain. Through it all, my dad was quietly at my side.

After 24-hours of agony and almost no sleep, a nurse rolled in a gurney and announed that it was time for me to have an MRI done. My parents protested. The nurse explained, "It's the only way to determine if the surgery was successful and what treatment he'll need."

Although it hurt to open my eyes, I looked up at my dad. He had tears in his eyes. He was the one that gently lifted me from the bed to the gurney. Dad held my head perfectly still as the attendants wheeled me down the hall. "I love you," he said to me again and again.

During the procedure, Dad quietly told me a story. "Imagine the two of us alone in a boat," he said, "floating on our favorite Wisconsin lake." For the first time since the surgery, I felt myself relaxing. Like a tightly wound coil that unwinds, the tension from the pain began to loosen. I felt myself soaking up love and strength from my dad's calm presence. Then, a most unlikely thing occured—as I slid into the hard and uncomfortable MRI tube, I drifted into a sound sleep.

My pain had been my dad's pain. I know he would have taken it all on himself if given the choice. It hurt him to realize the MRI would increase my discomfort, so he did everything in his power to overcome that. He surrounded me with all the strength and love he had.

A few weeks later, I left the hospital, fully recovered. Unfortunately, two years later, the tumor returned, requiring another surgery. But before I returned for my second surgery, my parents had an artist paint a picture of Aslan holding a young boy safe in his paws. That boy is me and Aslan is my dad. I love that painting. Just as Aslan's paws safely held the Narnians, my dad's gentle hands held me and comforted me, surrounding me with love.

And so do the hands of my Heavenly Father. He doesn't take away the pain and suffering that come with living in this world, but His strong and tender hands never cease to hold me tight.

—Daniel Daily

Daniel Daily grew up in Little Rock, Arkansas, where he underwent both of his brain surgeries, and later moved to Woodland Park, Colorado. He now attends college in Oklahoma and runs track. Daniel also loves snowboarding, rock climbing, hiking, camping, whitewater rafting, and many outside activities. In the summer, he works for Kanakuk Kamps in Colorado, where he's a counselor and a whitewater rafting guide.

Blindsided

I was writing a humor column about money and marriage when the phone rang. Letting it ring, I finished writing the sentence: "Someone stole my Visa card, but I haven't reported it yet. The thief is spending less than my wife." Then I picked up the receiver. There was silence at first, then my wife's voice, speaking the words I've never forgotten: "H-h-help me; please help me. I don't know what's happening ..."

Normally, it's a five-minute jog from my office to our house, but I'm sure I was there in two. Bursting through the front door, I found the kids on the kitchen floor pouring Corn Flakes into a stainless steel bowl. "Daddy, is Mamma gonna die?" asked the eldest, five-year-old Stephen.

On the living room couch lay Ramona, my wife of nine years. An ugly gash ran up her left leg, and blood had stained the carpet. Staring at me with vacant eyes, she asked, "What day is it? It's Monday, right?"

It was Friday, April 10, 1992. The first day of a journey down a road we would never have chosen.

Until that day, life had been everything we had hoped for. We'd had three kids in three years and we couldn't have been happier. I often joked with Ramona, "Sure we have three kids, but we're far more satisfied than the guy who has three million dollars."

"How so?" she asked.

"Well, the guy with three million wants more!"

We had a close family, an improving marriage, even a car that started. And my first book had just been accepted by a publisher.

Early in January 1992, however, things began to change. Waking up in the middle of the night, I'd find Ramona pacing the floor. "What's wrong?" I'd ask.

"I'm fine," she'd reply. "I just can't sleep."

Finally one night she broke down and told me, "I'm hardly sleeping. I'm thinking about this disease that's in my family."

The disease was Huntington's, a rare neurological disorder. On the scale of human misery, the disease ranks high, bringing mental and physical deterioration, then nursing homes and life support systems. "My dad had it before he drowned and I have a 50/50 chance of getting it," she had told me when we were dating. "I thought you should know, before we get ... any further along." My response was the last thing she expected: "I'd like to marry you someday, Ramona. I love you." After that I never gave the disease much thought. We were young—invincible.

But by the time our kids were born, three of Ramona's six siblings had been diagnosed with Huntington's, and she thought she was next. The symptoms were there: lack of sleep, irritability, occasional clumsiness, even a craving for sweets.

In the morning before the fateful phone call, my wife awoke at 8 a.m. feeling dizzy. The last thing she remembers is standing up to pull on her housecoat. As she fell, her leg struck the corner of our wooden bed frame.

I wrapped Ramona's wound and headed for the kitchen. "What happened to Mommy?" I asked Stephen, who was stirring the Corn Flakes while his two-year-old brother added a generous handful of salt.

"She was making funny noises," he answered, "and she didn't talk right. She thinks I'm her dad."

I gathered my three children into my arms and held them close. "Maybe we should tell Jesus," said Rachael, who was three. "Maybe he can do something." Squeezing them tightly, I prayed out loud: "Dear God, help Mommy to be OK. And thank You that You're here with us all the time."

"Daddy," said Rachael, pulling on my ear, "can we have breakfast now?"

As the children munched cold cereal, I called my parents. "Mom, I'm not sure what's wrong with Ramona. But can you take the kids for awhile—and pray?" Then I phoned Ramona's mother. Half an hour later she arrived with a hug. But her optimistic smile soon faded. "You're sure it's Friday?" Ramona kept asking. "It can't be."

I was flipping through a phone book for our doctor's number when suddenly Ramona's back arched and her head snapped back. An agonizing moan escaped her lips. Her face—an ashen gray—tightened, and her body slumped to the floor. Quickly I rolled her over to keep her from choking. "Dial 9-1-1!" I yelled. Ramona thrashed her arms and legs, but no breath would come. Grabbing her arms to keep her from hurting herself, I prayed, "Oh God, please, please ..." It was the first seizure I'd ever witnessed. It would be the first of hundreds.

An ambulance came to take Ramona to a hospital ninety minutes away. I rode with my unconscious wife, clutching her hand and wondering if this was the beginning of Huntington's. A Christian nurse, a childhood friend, was with us. "I once read an interview with Linda Ronstadt," I told her. "She said, 'I'll never get married; there's too much potential for pain.' I guess I finally understand what she meant."

My friend put her hand on mine. "Yes," she replied, "but you would never have known such joy either." I didn't bother wiping my tears away.

In the hospital, the endless battery of tests began. You name it, they scanned it. "They scanned my brain and found nothing?" joked Ramona on the morning of the fourth day. I laughed and kissed her. But the outlook wasn't so funny. Doctors, psychologists, and neurologists all had different opinions. "This has nothing to do with Huntington's," said one. "She's having pseudo-seizures. She'll get over it." A veteran psychologist told us that because Ramona had watched her father drown when she was eight, she had post-traumatic stress disorder. "Counseling is the answer," he told me.

Back home, our doctor diagnosed her with severe depression and recommended an anti-depressant. During the next few weeks Ramona seemed to improve. My boss allowed me to carry on my editorial duties at home, and at night after everyone was asleep I put the finishing touches on my book, *Honey, I Dunked the Kids*. In one chapter I told how our youngest son, Jeffrey, was born less than a year after his sister. "God's grace always accompanies life's surprises," I wrote. When Ramona's seizures returned with a vengeance, I hung onto those words.

In March of 1993, the gene that causes Huntington's was discovered at last. And so, one year after the seizures began, we drove to a nearby city for a simple blood test. "We'll be in touch," the nurse told us. But weeks of waiting turned to months. Finally I called the clinic. "Why so long?" I asked. "It's a little-known disease," came the response. "We're sorry."

In July my book came out, and I began doing radio interviews over the phone to promote it. "How can you laugh when life ain't so funny?" one talk show host asked. I talked about how our present days couldn't be described as happy ones, but strangely there were moments when they were jam-packed with joy. "Joy," I said, "doesn't depend on sunny circumstances, on good news or happy endings. It comes from knowing that whatever happens, God loves me; that whatever happens He's preparing a better place for those who love Him." During the commercials I'd take a break from the interview and run to the next room to check on my wife.

Early in 1994, we were notified that the test results had come back. On February 14th, we'd know whether Ramona carried the Huntington's gene. Valentine's Day is no occasion for final verdicts, I thought. Then I realized how fitting it was. On August 28, 1982, I had stood before 300 witnesses and God himself, promising to be Ramona's sweetheart no matter what came our way. On each Valentine's Day since I had renewed that vow. I would renew it this year just like before.

On February 14th, two doctors tore open the small envelope that held the test results. "Ramona, you have the normal gene."

We stood together in disbelief. "We don't have it?"

"You don't have it."

We hugged the doctors. Ramona was clear, and the disease could not be passed on to our children. That night we celebrated with a seafood dinner and a movie. Driving home we felt as if we'd come out of a long, dark tunnel. But we weren't out of it yet.

As the months dragged on, Ramona's seizures worsened. "Things will get better," our doctor kept telling us. "It just takes time." But by 1996, time seemed to be running out.

Down to a mere ninety pounds, Ramona had no appetite and rarely left the house. When she did, people in our small town barely recognized her. One day as we drove to visit her sister, another seizure laid her flat out in the front seat beside me. Terrified, the children cried in the back seat. I comforted them as best I could, and after our arrival, took them to a nearby McDonald's.

"How do you guys feel?" I asked.

"Scared," came the reply. "Is Mama gonna die?"

"I don't know," I said. "Sometimes I'm scared, too. But you know what? God said He'll always be with us. And He's never broken a promise. You can tell Him when you're scared. And you can tell me too, OK?" I didn't know if I'd said the right thing, but soon the kids were laughing and enjoying their cheeseburgers.

As a father, I wanted to protect my children from pain. Yet, I knew that pain was a part of life and I didn't get to chose when and how much my children would receive of it. All I could do was love them and be there for them. And I knew that God loved us and was there for us, even if he led us on a path that would not be easy.

We had seen twenty-one specialists, scoured libraries for literature, and tried to diagnose the problem ourselves. Well meaning friends suggested that demonic activity was involved, so we sought godly counsel.

Every night we lay awake, unable to sleep. And sometimes panic overtook me. "What do I do now, Lord? Where do we go from here?" There was only silence. The windows of heaven seemed shut, the drapes pulled. Then verses my mother had drummed into me when I was a child came back to comfort me. And I would say them out loud: "God is our refuge and strength, an everpresent help in trouble. Therefore we will not fear ... " (Psalm 46:1-2).

But by the fall of 1996, even hope was slipping from my grasp. The seizures were occurring daily and sometimes every half hour. I rarely left Ramona's side, and late one night, after she was finally asleep, I paced our darkened backyard and fell to my knees pounding the ground. "God," I cried, "I can't take it anymore. Please do something."

As I stood to my feet, a doctor's name came to mind. We attended the same church, but I'd never thought to ask his opinion. A few minutes later I had him on the phone. After listening to my description, he said simply: "I've seen this once before. It sounds like a rare chemical deficiency. Bring her to me first thing in the morning. There's a new drug to treat it."

I don't think I really believed in miracles before then. But within a week, Ramona was a different person. The seizures ended. Her eyes lit up with the sparkle that first attracted me to her. God had given me my wife back.

Every day my wife wakes up beside the most thankful guy in the world. I'm thankful that God's grace does accompany life's surprises. I'm thankful that in the toughest of times His grace can help us choose joy over bitterness, and help us stay together when our whole world is falling apart.

—Phil Callaway

Phil Callaway is the best-selling author of fifteen books. His list of accomplishments also includes shutting off the television to listen to his children's questions (twice), taking out the garbage without being told (once), and convincing his high school sweetheart to marry him (once). Described as "Dave Barry with a message," Callaway is a popular speaker for corporations, conferences, camps, and marriage retreats. The Callaways live in Alberta, Canada. For info on Phil's books, new DVD, speaking engagements, and a complimentary fruitcake best before Christmas of '83, visit www.philcallaway.com

Dad, I'm So Glad You're Here

My son, Jacob, just had to go to the bathroom. It should have been simple. But then again, nothing had ever really been simple for Jacob.

Jacob was nine years old and had been battling osteosarcoma, a bone cancer, for nearly three years. After his first nine months of chemotherapy and three major surgeries, he had been in remission for eigtheen months before his cancer returned with a vengeance just before Christmas of 2001. That Yuletide surgery claimed a third of his right lung. Four months later, the cancer spread to his lower spinal column, causing excruciating back and leg pain. By late June, my wife, Cathy, and I knew Jacob was dying. The only treatment left for him was palliative treatment, but despite the doctors' assurances that "we can control his pain so he doesn't have to suffer," Jacob baffled the whole medical pain control establishment with his unique combination of physical and mental challenges.

For one thing, the cancer in his spine was in a location that made any further surgery a dicey proposition at best. The cancer's pressure on Jacob's spine, however, gave him constant, scaring pain that was only to become worse as he neared death. These physical difficulties were compounded by Jacob's being saddled with Asperger's Syndrome, a form of autism. For him, one of the many manifestations of Asperger's was an acute sensitivity to pain. Whatever pain a "normal" child would have felt was multiplied for Jacob, and he was not shy about expressing it.

It was our second day at Riley Children's Hospital in Indianapolis where we had brought Jacob in an attempt to get his mounting pain under control. The oral morphine doses we were administering at home were not doing the trick. All afternoon Jacob had been under total anesthesia so that he could lie still on his back to get a radiation treatment and a new MRI. His spinal pain prevented him from lying on his back while conscious, so they had to put him to sleep, and when he woke up from the anesthesia, he was in agony from having been supine for so long, anesthesia or no.

That pain, multiplied by Asperger's, then fed into another, more endearing characteristic of Jacob's autism— his quirkily fascinating use of language. My boy was quite the wordsmith. He sometimes described his pain as a "shadowy, gloomy, and gruesome prison," or would say "My bones feel like glass." On this particular occasion at Riley, the doctors, nurses, and I were all frantically trying to find the right combination of drugs to ease his pain, even while we tried to hold him down to keep him from thrashing and making it worse.

In his hurt, panic, and anger, Jacob shouted some vicious verbal barbs at us, his woefully inept pain team. "Why must you be so brutal?!" "You're all trying to kill me!" "Why must you torture me to death?" Despite the closed door, I'm sure his screams must have echoed down the hall of the children's cancer ward.

Finally, after what seemed like hours, the pain specialists were able to get enough narcotics into Jacob to get him to settle down. My poor little man was a wreck. Every muscle and sinew in his skinny, cancer-battered body was tensed like steel cable. He had urinated all over himself under anesthesia, so he reeked of urine and sweat, his bed sheets were soaked, and now he had to pee again. It should have been simple for a sick little boy to go to the bathroom, but every movement at this point was like nails driven into his flesh. He and I were alone in the room by this time. I lifted him out of bed as gently as I could, sat his stark naked body on my knee as I knelt with my other knee on the floor, and held his plastic urinal in place for him while I supported his upper body to keep him from falling over.

All of a sudden, just when I was feeling like the meanest, most useless father in the world for contributing to his torture, Jacob made a Herculean effort to raise his left arm enough to put it around me, leaned against me, and hugged me as tight as he possibly could. He pressed his head into my head and shoulder and said to me in a labored whisper, "Oh, Dad, I'm so glad you're here! You're the best, Dad!" I couldn't even hope to hold back my tears any more, and I just wept and said, "Oh, Jacob, I love you so much!" "I love *you*, Dad," was his reply, and we just held each other silently for a while.

That moment is one I'll treasure for the rest of my days, and it was certainly the moment I had to recall again and again every time I had to move Jacob or shift his body into positions that caused him pain, all the way up until he died a month and a day later. When he would yell at me for hurting him, I just had to remember that it was his pain talking, not my boy, and that I think what he really would have said if he could was "Oh, Dad, I'm so glad you're here!"

As for me, I guess that's the way I feel about God sometimes. I wondered why he allowed Jacob to hurt so much. I can find good intellectual and theological answers for that but it certainly didn't make it much easier to take at the time. Sometimes when Cathy and I would share Jacob's pain we just wanted to yell at God in our senselessness and say, "Why must you torture us?" just as Jacob used to scream at us.

But there's no doubt that, at the end of the day, when I'm hurting and exhausted and I reek of sin and frustration and doubt, God holds me on His lap and lets me rest, and that's when I come to my senses and bury my head in His shoulder and say, "Oh, Dad, I'm so glad you're here! You're the best, Dad!"

—Rex Rund

Rex Rund served with the Peace Corps in Haiti for three years. He is husband to Cathy and the father of three children—one who has gone to his heavenly home. The Runds live in the country near Sheridan, Indiana, where they garden, raise chickens, and enjoy each other's company. Rex serves as director of music and liturgy at Our Lady of Mt. Carmel Catholic Church in Carmel, Indiana, and Cathy is music director of the neighboring parish, St. Maria Goretti.

We've Come a Million Miles

I went weak with fear as I watched my husband, Steve, taken from the ambulance. "I'm here, Steve," I cried out. "Everything is going to be all right." But seeing his completely still body with blood coming out of his nose and ears, I trembled in horror.

Steve lay in a coma after plunging eight feet, head first, onto a concrete floor while at work as a warehouse manager. "We only had six years together ... just six short years," I cried. "What will my boys do without their Daddy?" It was all a surreal nightmare to me. "How could this be happening to us?"

The day had started like any other. After sharing breakfast with our two boys, Leyton, four, and Landon, three, Steve hugged us all good-bye and left for work. I took Leyton to preschool and Landon to daycare before going to my own job as operations manager for an investment company. Steve had called during the day to say hi and suggest meeting for lunch. "Sorry, it's so busy," I had apologized.

"OK; I'll see you at home," he promised.

But a few hours later, I answered a call from Billy, one of Steve's co-workers. "There's been an accident. You'd better get to the hospital."

"Steve's going to be all right, isn't he?" I asked. Steve was always so tough; never getting sick and never making a big deal out of getting hurt.

There was a pause. "I don't know," was Billy's reply. I went weak with fear. Something big must have happened. I jumped in the car and drove to the hospital, all the while pleading with God to spare my husband and my two boys' Daddy.

I met the ambulance at Trinity Hospital's emergency room and ran behind as Steve was wheeled away. As I entered the doors, I recognized the chaplain walking toward me. "No! Not this!" I cried out in anger. "Are you here because Steve is going to die?"

I wanted to fix things. Steve could not die and I did not want anyone telling me that he would.

I broke down sobbing and screaming. "Steve is such a loving husband and father," I cried. "My boys won't even remember him. How can we go on without him?"

Family and friends soon began to gather at the hospital. Two doctors took me aside to explain the situation. Steve's punctured lung and broken collar bone could have been fixed but his skull was fractured in several places. There was a large blood clot on the left side of his brain and his brain was bleeding.

"With or without surgery the outcome is going to be the same," was the solemn diagnosis.

"But he's going to be all right, right?" I asked desperately. The doctors looked helplessly at each other. I repeated the question. "But he's going to be all right?"

"No," one of the doctors whispered.

I became hysterical, curling up into a ball and putting my head between my legs. Through my sobs, I looked up the doctors. "You have to do surgery," I pleaded desperately.

Surgery would be futile, they explained. Steve's brain had swelled to the point that his skull could not accommodate it. It had begun to push down on the small opening at the base of the skull, damaging the brain stem. On a scale of zero to five for response, Steve was a zero. It was too late. Death would come quickly.

"But I want you to do surgery," I begged again through my tears. "Please!"

Both doctors looked at each other and then at me. "OK, but we need to move fast."

I insisted on seeing Steve one last time. Lying on the table surrounded by medical people, I cried to him, "Steve, it's going to be OK." Then, pleading with everyone around him, I begged, "Will you please make him better?" Everyone looked away.

In the waiting room, surrounded by family and friends, I cried out over and over, "Dear God, please please, please ..." Once the surgery had begun, a neurosurgeon—not involved in the operation—came into the waiting room. "I don't know what kind of believers you are, but I do believe and I've seen what prayer can do. Prayer is what you have left."

I hugged him and thanked him for his comforting words. Then, three hours later, another doctor delivered very grave news. "We did all we could but he's about as brain dead as he can be."

Again, I broke down. But this time I was resigned. In my mind I had begun planning the funeral and imagined the unthinkable—life without my beloved husband, raising our two boys alone. Around fifteen people were still there, including the pastor from my church. At that point, he stood up. "Dear Lord, we've been told that we need a miracle. I'm going to be brave enough to ask you for that miracle right now."

People prayed together and offered their presence so I would not have to wait alone. In spite of being surrounded by people, I felt so very alone faced with the prospect of our future without a husband and father. An hour later, a doctor again entered the room. I braced myself for the news that Steve had died.

"We were wrong," the doctor smiled cautiously. "Steve's responding. He has a million miles to go, but he has a chance."

I could not believe my ears. "Do you think he's responding?" I gasped.

"No," the doctor announced, "I *know* he's responding."

It took a moment for the euphoria of this immense news to sink in. My husband had been brought back from the dead. Tears of joy and hugs filled the room. He was going to live!

Steve was taken to ICU to be kept sedated for four days to begin healing. But after only three days, he woke up. "Do you know your name is Steve?" I asked. He nodded. "Do you know you have two boys?" Again Steve nodded. My husband was still with me! On Monday, Leyton and Landon came to see their Daddy. Steve's eyes lit up and he smiled. "Here's my guys," he called out and gave them a big hug.

"I love you, Daddy!" the boys cried.

Initially there were many gaps in his memory. Steve spent another two weeks in ICU and three more in rehabilitation before leaving for a special traumatic brain injury outpatient program in Texas for three more months in therapy. He returned home on March 4, 2005, and was back to work at his old job just one month later.

We have also gone through extensive marital counseling. We learned that only ten percent of marriages survive traumaic brain injury because it often changes the injured spouses's personality. Also, Steve lost much of his hearing and partial vision in his left eye and has had to work hard to be the independent person he was before. So, the work has not just been with him, it has been with me, too. We've had to rebuild our relationship and begin anew.

We really have come a million miles. It has been a long and often difficult journey that we are still on through the grace of God. Once the euphoria of his survival died down and people went back to their own routines, there was just Steve and me and the kids. And of course, God. I know that God saved Steve for a reason. I believe that God answered our prayers and kept our family together. When the boys are with their Daddy and I hear that laughter that goes clear down to their toes, I just cry tears of joy. I remember: this is why I wanted him to live so much.

—Christie Lang

It has been two year's since the accident and Christie says she feels like they've passed the million mile marker long ago. Steve still works for West Central and works even harder than he did before. He still struggles with memory loss, hearing loss, and loss of sight in one eye. These disabilities, however, don't interfere with his joy of fatherhood. Leyton and Landon are now five and six and are still his two biggest fans.

Chapter 3
A Father's Faithfulness

A Miracle of Mermaids

"I miss you so much, Daddy," whispered four-year-old Desiree Gill through silent tears as she traced her finger along the face of her father in a framed photograph set on the coffee table. "Why did you leave me?" The tiny girl stared at the smiling image of her father, Ken, remembering all their good times together.

The Gills had lived happily in a small two-bedroom bungalow in the rural suburbs of Yuba City, California. Standing six-foot-three with a muscular build, Ken was a gentle giant whom everyone loved. However, it was no secret that his biggest passion was his daughter. "Nothing can keep me and my girl apart," Ken had always said. Then, in January of 1993, Ken seriously injured his back at work and died suddenly from complications.

"Daddy's gone to heaven to be with Jesus," Desiree's mother tried to explain each time her daughter asked for Ken. However, Desiree had her own ideas. "I know where Daddy is. He's at work. He'll be home soon," she insisted.

Rhonda sighed as she stepped into the living room and once again found her daughter lost in memories. "Desi," Rhonda said softly as she embraced her daughter, "You know Daddy always loved you and he would be with you if he could." Desiree opened her hand to reveal a hair ornament made of fishing line and tape that she had been clutching. "Daddy made this the day he bought me my own fishing rod," she sobbed.

As the weeks and months passed, Desiree's grief did not abate. Instead, she became quieter and more withdrawn. Desiree was particularly distressed on the day that would have marked her father's twenty-ninth birthday, November 8, 1993. "How will I send him a birthday card?" Desiree asked her grandmother, Trish. "He'll think I forgot."

Trish proposed an idea: "How 'bout we tie a letter to a balloon and send it up to Daddy in heaven?" Desiree's eyes lit up at the simple logic.

With the backseat of Trish's car loaded with flowers for their gravesite celebration, Desiree, her mother, and grandmother stopped at a local supermarket to buy a balloon. Desiree instantly chose a silver "Happy Birthday" balloon with a picture of the Little Mermaid from the Disney film, which was her favorite video to watch with her father.

A very light breeze rippled the eucalyptus trees as the three spread their picnic lunch alongside Ken's grave. Desiree was so excited that she could barely sit still in the grass as she dictated a letter to her dad. "Tell him 'Happy Birthday.' I love you and miss you," she rattled off, "I hope you have a good birthday since this is your first one with Jesus. I hope you get this and can write me on my birthday in January…" Rhonda and Trish wrapped the letter in plastic and tied it to the end of the balloon's string. Then, the three said a little prayer for Jesus to take care of Ken, and Desiree sent her message off to heaven.

Desiree watched the silver balloon as it sailed toward the Pacific Ocean. Finally, Rhonda and Trish decided it was time to pack up and go home. "Now Dad's going to write me back," Desiree declared with utter certainty as she walked past them toward the car.

❧

On a cold rainy November morning on Prince Edward Island, Canada, Wade MacKinnon dressed in his waterproof gear to go duck hunting. Wade and his young family lived in the small community of Mermaid, just east of the island's capital, Charlottetown. Wildlife was plentiful around the MacKinnon's rural home, so rather than heading to the estuary where he usually hunted, he decided on a whim to go to tiny Mermaid Lake.

As Wade and his longtime hunting companion Zack, a black Labrador retriever, emerged from the backwoods into the cranberry bog surrounding the lake, there was not a duck to be seen. However, something fluttered from the bushes on the shoreline and caught his eye. Curious, Wade approached to find a partially deflated balloon snagged in the branches. Printed on the silver lining was a picture of a mermaid. When he untangled the string he found a soggy piece of paper wrapped in plastic at the end. Since there were no ducks, Wade decided to head back home and take the balloon to his eighteen-month-old daughter.

Once home, Wade detached the note from the string and laid it on the kitchen counter to dry. An hour later his wife, Donna, came in from shopping and together they read the note dated November 8, 1993. "Happy Birthday Daddy ..." It finished with a mailing address in Live Oak, California. Wade shook his head in disbelief, "I can't believe this came all the way from California. It's only the twelfth of November. This balloon traveled almost 4,300 miles in just four days. That's more than 1,000 miles a day!"

"And look!" Donna turned the balloon over, "This is a Little Mermaid balloon and it landed at Mermaid Lake." She shuddered and whispered, "What a strange coincidence."

"We have to write Desiree," Wade exclaimed. "Maybe we were chosen to help this little girl." But as soon as he looked at his wife, he knew she didn't feel the same way. Donna had tears in her eyes and was stepping away from the balloon. "You have to take this back where you found it. It's not right that we have this in our house," she said in a trembling voice. "Such a young girl having to deal with death ... it's so awful."

Wade felt Donna's sadness, too, but at the same time he marveled at the faith of this young girl to send a balloon aloft in search of a message from her father. Wade knew there was no point arguing with his wife. He would simply wait a few days until she had time to think it over. In the meantime, he placed the note in a drawer and tied the still floating balloon to the railing of the balcony overlooking their living room.

Over the next two weeks, the MacKinnons' four-month-old son developed an ear infection that would wake him throughout the night. To comfort him, Donna would take him downstairs and hold him stretched out nearly upright on her chest as she reclined on the couch. It was the only position that would relieve some of his congestion and help him sleep. As she lay groggily staring, the balloon caught her eye. Bobbing eerily in the semi-darkness, it made her uncomfortable. "Are you a bad omen?" Donna asked it. "Did you bring my baby's ear infection?"

"That's it," she vowed one night, and the next morning she stuffed the balloon out of sight in a closet. However, as the days and weeks passed, Donna found herself thinking more and more about the balloon. "It flew over the Rocky

Mountains, across the Great Lakes," she couldn't help marveling. "Just a few more miles and it would have landed in the ocean." Instead, though, the note from the tormented little girl who couldn't understand why her beloved father had been taken from her had come into Wade and Donna's life. "Our children are so lucky," she thought. "They have two healthy parents. Imagine how one of them would feel if Wade were to die."

Over coffee the following morning, as Wade readied for work, Donna firmly told him, "You're right. We have this balloon for a reason. I don't know what it is, but we have to try to help Desiree." Wade just smiled and hugged his wife. He suspected all along that she'd come around.

In a bookstore in downtown Charlottetown, Donna bought a copy of the Hans Christian Anderson book, *The Little Mermaid*. A few days later, just after Christmas, Wade returned home with a birthday card. It read, "For a Dear Daughter, Loving Birthday Wishes." "That's an odd card to send her," Donna mused. Wade insisted, "It's her daddy, not us, who's sending the gift. We must not pretend to be taking his place." After spending days thinking and consulting with her husband, Donna finally sat down one morning to write. Desiree had said her birthday was in January and the MacKinnons wanted the card and gift to arrive in time. Donna thought it would be difficult to compose an intimate letter to a perfect stranger just four years old on the other end of the continent, but once she put pen to paper the sentences seemed to flow effortlessly, as if she was writing to a long lost friend. She explained how they had found Desiree's balloon and that they lived in a community called Mermaid. Tucking the letter into the birthday card along with the book, she took the package to the post office and mailed it to California on January 3, 1994.

꧁

"Do you think Daddy has my balloon yet?" Desiree would needle her mother every day. "When will he write back?" Rhonda noticed that Desiree had changed since they had sent the balloon. Now she was not only melancholy, she was also impatient and restless to hear from her father. "Oh, Mom," Rhonda confided to Trish, "I'm scared we did the wrong thing with this balloon thing. We seem to have gotten her hopes up so. What will we do when she doesn't get her answer?" They discussed at length possibilities—such as sending up another balloon or even faking a return letter— but in the end they decided to simply let time take over.

Desiree's fifth birthday came and went quietly with a small party on January 9, 1994, with no reply from her father. She stopped asking questions, and spent more and more time by herself. It seemed as though her pain had become internalized.

Ten days later, a brown manila envelope arrived for Desiree at her grandmother's house. She did not recognize the return address and assumed it was from one of Ken's relatives. Later that evening, her curiosity piqued as she thought about the package. She decided it would be best to find out what was inside before handing it over to her young granddaughter.

It was after midnight when the telephone woke Rhonda out of a deep sleep. "Oh, Rhonda. I can't believe it," Trish sobbed from the other end. "Desi got her answer from Ken. Listen, listen," and she began to read. "Mom!" Rhonda interrupted, "I can't understand a word. Bring it over first thing in the morning."

At the crack of dawn, Trish pulled into Rhonda's driveway. Rhonda and Desiree had awakened early and were expecting her. Rhonda had told her daughter that a letter arrived from her father, and Desiree surprised her mother with a matter-of-fact reply: "I know."

Desiree sat on the couch between her mother and grandmother, who tearfully handed over the package. "Here Grandma," Desiree said calmly, as she held out the birthday card, "read it to me." Trish began: "Happy birthday from your daddy. I guess you must be wondering who we are. Well, it all started in early December when my husband, Wade, went duck hunting. Guess what he found? No, it wasn't a duck, it was a mermaid balloon that you sent your daddy ..." Trish paused. A single tear began to trickle down Desiree's cheek. "There are no stores in heaven so your daddy wanted someone to do his shopping for him. I think he picked us because we live in a town called Mermaid and our oldest daughter's birthday is also in January ..." Trish read on. "I know your daddy would want you to be happy and not to be sad. I know he loves you very much and will always be watching over you. Lots of love, the MacKinnons."

The three generations of females embraced each other as they cried tears of joy and sorrow. Desiree blurted out: "I knew Daddy would find a way not to forget me." Desiree's conviction caused her mother and grandmother to gaze at one another with a look that seemed to say, "How pathetic that we are filled with doubts and questions, while this little girl's dreams came true simply because she believed."

When Trish read the Hans Christian Anderson version of *The Little Mermaid* to her granddaughter she was alarmed by the ending, which was strikingly different from the Disney edition. In the Disney tale, the Little Mermaid lives happily ever after with the handsome prince. In the book the MacKinnons sent, the Little Mermaid, unable to kill the prince so that he can join her at the bottom of the sea, returns home, but drowns because a curse from the wicked witch will not allow her to have her mermaid's tail. Rhonda and Trish were shaken, but Desiree put her hands on her cheeks with wide-eyed delight. "She goes to heaven," Desiree said with reverence. "That's why Daddy sent me this book, because the mermaid goes to heaven just like him."

The MacKinnons' goodwill had an instant affect on Desiree. Although the death of her father caused her to mature and to lose some of her carefree, child-like innocence, Desiree's cheerful, openhearted personality returned. She now understood where he was and that he was still with her, loving her. Desiree is at peace.

A month after Desiree received her package, Donna MacKinnon's hands trembled as she opened a thick letter addressed to her family. It was sent from California. Donna could hardly believe how involved she had become in this strange, fairytale-like scenario that had so unexpectedly burst into their lives. Donna was flooded with relief as she read what Rhonda had written, "There are no words to express how special your family is except to say that you were surely heaven sent. On January 19 my prayers were answered and my little girl's dream came true when your parcel arrived. When we read your letter she cried with happiness ..."

Newspapers and television stations picked up the story. Since garnering attention in the media, Desiree has been getting mail from as far away as the Philippines. She has received gifts from strangers, even prisoners, who have heard her heart-warming story.

Desiree and her mother have developed a friendship with the MacKinnon's. "People often say, 'What a coincidence your mermaid balloon landed so far away at a place called

Mermaid Lake!'" says Rhonda, "But we know better. We know her dad picked the MacKinnons as a way to keep sending his love to Desiree."

—Margo Pfeiff

Margo Pfeiff is an award-winning freelance writer and photographer based in Montreal. A writing instructor at conferences, she has been a special correspondent with Reader's Digest *since 1992 and written for numerous books and other publications including the* Los Angeles Times, San Francisco Chronicle, National Post, *and* Globe & Mail. *Currently, Margo is working on a book about contemporary life in the Canadian territory of Nunavut.*

The Saving Sign

My father was a Marine who served during World War II. For the most part, Dad rarely spoke about the war. Like most soldiers who served, the subject was one with too many painful memories. Dad generally kept the subject light and entertaining whenever he did speak about it. There was one story, though, that my father loved to tell my brothers and me whenever we asked him about the war.

During the winding down of the war against Japan, Dad served in the Pacific. One night, he drew night patrol and was assigned to scout for enemy troop movements in the rough jungle terrain. He had just climbed a tree to conceal himself, when seemingly out of nowhere, the entire area beneath the tree was filled with Japanese soldiers. Dad found himself trapped in the treetop for hours, as the enemy decided to camp right beneath the tree.

Barely able to breath for fear of giving away his position, Dad said he spent the time praying for God's protection and asking God to help him. Every prayer he had ever learned swirled through his mind and heart as he waited silently in that treetop. He prayed not to be discovered. And as time went on, he began to pray for the enemy soldiers beneath the tree. He said he could see in his minds eye our family back home, and he imagined these soldiers were missing their loved ones, too.

Up close, the enemy soldiers looked very much like the men in his unit. While their physical appearance was different and he could not understand their language, he knew that they were God's children, too. They were all men caught up in a war, which had brought them all to serve their respective countries. They fought for what they thought was right according to their upbringing and nationality. Like him, they were ordinary men—some with children—who might never see their loved ones again should they perish in the jungles of war. As he prayed and watched them, they sat relaxed around the jungle clearing, laughing and sharing letters and photos from back home, just as my father and his fellow soldiers often did.

As night began to give way to the first light of the morning, my father accepted that in the end he would probably not be returning home. The odds were stacked against him. He knew he could not remain motionless and undetected for much longer. Having made his peace with God, my dad began his final silent prayer. He prayed for the men beneath the tree and their families and for courage for himself.

Just as my father gave everything over to our Father in heaven and made the sign of the cross, an enemy soldier spotted his hiding place in the treetop. As my father signed himself with the cross, their eyes locked. To my dad's utter amazement, the enemy soldier silently made the sign of the cross himself, and put his finger to his lips as if to say, "Be still my brother. I shall not betray you." Almost in that very instant, the enemy soldiers began to move out as silently and as quickly as they had arrived.

My dad never ceased thanking God for his protection on that day. And Dad always remembered to pray for his brother in Christ—an enemy soldier, whose name he never knew—who had spared his life and surely loved God, too.

—Christine Trollinger

Christine Trollinger's biography appears after "Daddy's Little Girl" in Chapter 1 – A Father's Love.

God Looks After His Own

One winter's morning in 1931, I came down to breakfast—and found the table empty of food.

It was cold. Outside in Kalamazoo, Michigan, the worst blizzard on record had paralyzed the city. No cars were out. The snow had drifted up two stories high against our house, blackening the windows.

"Daddy, what's happening?" I asked.

I was six years old. Gently, Dad told me our fuel and food supplies were exhausted. He'd just put the last piece of coal on the fire. Mother had eight ounces of milk left for my baby brother, Tom. After that, nothing.

"So, what are we going to eat?" I said.

"We'll have our devotions first, John Edmund," he said, in a voice that told me I should not ask questions.

My father was a pastor. As a Christian believer, he'd been chased out of his Syrian homeland. He arrived as a teenager in the United States with no money and barely a word of English—nothing but his vocation to preach. He knew a kind of hardship few see today. Yet my parents consistently gave away at least ten percent of their income, and no one but God ever knew when we were in financial need.

That morning, Dad read from the Scriptures, as usual, and afterward we knelt for prayer. He prayed earnestly for the family, for our relatives and friends, for those he called the "missionaries of the cross," and those in the city who'd endured the blizzard without adequate shelter.

Then he prayed something like this:

"Lord, Thou knowest we have no more coal to burn. If it can please Thee, send us some fuel. If not, Thy will be done. We thank Thee for warm clothes and bed covers that will keep us comfortable even without the fire. Also, Thou knowest we have no food except milk for Baby Thomas. If it can please Thee..."

For someone facing bitter cold and hunger, he was remarkably calm. Nothing deflected him from completing the family devotions—not even the clamor we now heard beyond the muffling wall of snow.

Finally, someone pounded on the door. The visitor had cleared the snow off the window pane, and we could see his face peering in.

"Your door's iced up," he yelled. "I can't open it."

The devotions over, Dad jumped up. He pulled; the man pushed. When the door suddenly gave, an avalanche of slow fell into the entrance hall. I didn't recognize the man, and I don't think Dad did either, because he said politely, "Can I help you?"

The man explained he was a farmer who'd heard Dad preach in the city of Allegan three years earlier.

"I awakened at four o'clock this morning," he said, "and I couldn't get you out of my mind. The truck was stuck in the garage, so I harnessed the horses to the sleigh and came over."

"Well, please come in," my father said. On any other occasion he'd have added, "and have some breakfast with us." But, of course, today there was no breakfast.

The man thanked him. And then—to our astonishment—he plucked a large box off the sleigh. More than sixty years later, I can see that box as clear as yesterday. It contained milk, eggs, butter, pork chops, grain, homemade bread, and a host of other things. When the farmer had delivered the box, he went back out and got a cord of wood.

Finally, after a very hearty breakfast, he insisted Dad take a ten-dollar bill.

Almost every day, Dad reminded us that "God is the Provider." And my experience throughout my adult life has confirmed that in God's economy, those who give without stinting receive without limit. As it says in Psalm 37:25, "I have never seen the righteous forsaken nor God's seed begging bread." The Bible said it. But Dad and Mom showed me it was true.

—John Edmund Haggai

Dr. John Edmund Haggai is the founder of Haggai Institute for Advanced Leadership Training, based in Atlanta, Georgia, with international training centers located in Singapore and Maui, Hawaii.

The Dream

When I first got married, I often told people that my wife, Patti, and I would have eight to ten kids. She thought I was joking.

Two years into our marriage our first son, Aaron, was born; followed by Luke, and then Tyler, all two years apart. They were three balls of energy and, admittedly, Patti did the bulk of childcare. I looked forward to more children, but Patti informed me that three were enough, at least for the time being.

We were Catholics who went to church most Sundays, but we were not terribly concerned about Catholic teaching on family planning. To top it off, our parish priest in Montana was also a doctor who purported, "It's not reasonable to expect Catholic couples in today's world to follow the Church's teaching on contraception."

I was not too concerned about Catholic teaching myself— I just wanted more children. What was I to do? I started praying to God that the pills Patti was taking would fail. They did. Patti laughed when I told her I had been praying behind her back and my prayers had been answered. Even though we had not planned for another child at that time, Patti did love babies and could not help but feel love and joy for our unborn child. But in the midst of all this, I was laid off at my job as a radio news announcer. I had to look for work with the pressure of a pregnant wife, no insurance, and three small boys. We were in a difficult situation, but came to understand that our life was in God's hands. We prayed, waited, and trusted. Then, a job offer came from Bismarck, North Dakota.

A few months later, our son, Jacob, was born on the feast of Our Lady of Fatima, May 13th. This was also my birthday and Mother's Day that year. I had been born on Mother's Day thirty-four years earlier.

While in North Dakota, we started attending Mass regularly and Patti began to read a book about Marian apparitions around the world. We started to pray the Rosary together. Still, it took a while for us to get from point "A" to point "Z." We were on the road to becoming better Catholics, but we still had a way to go, especially when it came to family planning.

"Mark, we have four boys under the age of eight. Maybe we can adopt someday and be open to children that way," Patti told me one night. "But I do not think it is reasonable for me to have more. It is only fair that you get a vasectomy."

I protested that getting surgically altered was against Church teaching. Since people talked about getting sterilized as nonchalantly as they discussed getting a tooth filled, Patti insisted that I was being overly dramatic. I relented.

But as Patti grew in her faith and kept reading, she came to the conclusion that since the Church had never veered from its teaching against contraception for 2,000 years, perhaps it was right and she had been wrong. The desire to do God's will, whatever that meant, grew in her. She confided in me that she had been wrong to pressure me to have a vasectomy. "Oh great," I said. "*Now* you figure it out." Then I accused her, "You were Eve."

"Well," she said thoughtfully, "I guess I was. But Adam was kicked out of the Garden of Eden, too, so you're not off the hook."

Patti and I decided that we did want more children, in whatever way God willed for us, be it through adoption or birth. Since stories of failed vasectomies abound, we figured that praying for God's will would cover us.

Then, one day, when I returned home from work, Patti asked me to sit down. This was not the routine, so I braced myself. "I think you should get a reversal," she began. I jumped out of my seat and shouted, "No way. You talked me into one surgery, but I'm not going to have another. The subject is closed."

I refused to even consider a reversal. I clung to the belief that I had prayed our way out of the birth control pills, so we could pray our way out of this as well. So, for several months I prayed that we would have more children in spite of my self-imposed sterility. Then, one Sunday morning, I awoke with a change of heart. In the bustle of getting our crew out the door to church, I kept it to myself.

Over breakfast, after Mass, I casually wondered out loud how much a reversal operation would cost. Patti blurted out in great detail everything about a reversal.

"How do you know so much about reversals?" I asked.

"I had called the doctor's office to find out about it, but you had refused to even consider it," she answered.

"I cannot get time off from work this month, but I can go next month, in January," I stated.

Patti's eyes opened wide in astonishment. "But Mark, what changed your mind?" she asked.

"I had a dream last night. There were two babies in it. I believe that God was showing me the babies He had planned for us." The dream had evoked a love for these babies as strong as the love I had for my other children.

Patti looked stunned and gasped. "Mark, I had that same dream," she revealed. "That is the reason I asked you to get a reversal. I saw two babies—one dark-haired and one light—and felt an intense love for them as if they were my babies. When I woke up, I believed that God had planned those babies for us, but because of our sin, they would never be born. Since you would not consider a reversal, I decided I would put it in God's hands and let Him handle it."

One month after the reversal, we were expecting a new baby. Patti had a strong feeling that it would be our first girl and that God wanted us to name her Mary after the Blessed Mother, who had intervened for us. We had never considered the name before. She wrote on a slip of paper, "Yes, I think Mary would be a good name," and tucked it her wallet. When I suggested the name Mary—without knowing she had thought of it, too—she pulled out the slip of paper. We both believe that God desired that we honor Mary by naming our first girl after her.

Our blond-haired baby girl was born on December 22, 1993. Dark-haired Teresa was born on Patti's birthday, April 18, 1996.

Patti thought we must be done now that we had the babies from our dream. As usual, I said I thought ten would be a good number of children. "Maybe God just showed us two so as not to scare you," I joked.

Patti decided to pray and ask God if he wanted us to have more. While praying one day, she recalled that when St. Maximilian Kolbe was young, he had received a vision of our Blessed Mother. She had shown him two wreaths of roses: one of red, representing martyrdom, and one of white, representing purity. She asked him which one he would like to choose. He asked if he could choose both. Patti wondered, if like St. Maximilian, should we be willing to take on more than God asked? We both prayed for guidance.

John was born on August 31, 1999, and Isaac was born on his sister Mary's birthday, December 22, 2001. There could be no greater blessing on our family than our precious children. I often look at the four youngest and shudder to think of what we would have missed had we not sought God's will in our lives.

Patti became pregnant one more time. Matthew never made it into this world, but we believe he will be the first to greet us when we leave this one. We also were blessed with taking in two wonderful AIDS orphans—Joash and Calvin—from Kenya to fulfill my dream of having eight to ten kids! The Lord truly works in mysterious ways.

—Mark Armstrong

Mark Armstrong is a co-editor of Amazing Grace for Fathers. *His biography appears at the end of the book.*

Chicken Runs at Midnight

As third base coach for the Pittsburgh Pirates in 1992, I felt like I was on top of the world. Although it was only March, it was obvious we had a strong team and could expect a winning season.

But with one phone call, my world suddenly shattered. "Dad, I have something to tell you," my seventeen-year-old daughter, Amy, began. "Don't be mad at me."

With an opening like that, a hundred possibilities crossed my mind: she wrecked the car; drugs; pregnancy; bad grades ... "What is it?" I asked, impatient for the bad news.

"Dad, I have a brain tumor."

I froze. *No!* I could not be hearing right. *Not a brain tumor. Not my "Ames."*

"Dad, I'm sorry," she said breaking the silence.

"Sorry? What do you have to be sorry for?" I choked into the receiver.

But that was Amy. She was thinking about her dad rather than herself.

As the only girl among three brothers, Amy grew up to be one tough kid. When she was little, she loved to have me ask her: "Where do you want to go today?" Then, wherever she answered, I'd throw her giggling across the room onto the bed followed by the inevitable plea of, "Do it again, Daddy!"

But underneath her softly freckled face and strawberry blonde hair beat a heart of gold. Often I came home to find our garage full of neighborhood children playing school with Amy. She loved kids and dreamed of being a school teacher one day.

My season with the Pirates was bittersweet that year. Her mother and I had divorced years earlier, but Amy and her brothers—Bubba, Mike, and Tim—usually spent the summers with me. That year, her illness and chemotherapy weakened her so much that she needed to stay home in Arlington, Texas.

Still, we talked often. Amy was my number one fan. Baseball meant a lot to her because it meant a lot to me. Even though she could not come to the games, she decorated the house with orange and black pom poms, wore Pirate t-shirts and watched the games on television. We missed each other so much.

When the Pirates won the national championship that year, Amy flew out to attend the fifth game of the playoffs with the Atlanta Braves. It was not easy—her body weakened from chemotherapy, her head bald—but she was still full of life as she cheered enthusiastically. Winning this game was the icing on the cake of having my number one fan there.

After the game, Amy leaned over while I was driving the car and asked, "Dad, when there's a man at second and you get down in your stance and cup your hands, what are you telling him? 'Chicken runs at midnight?'"

I laughed so hard I almost drove off the road. "Chicken runs at midnight? Where did you come up with that?" I asked.

Amy laughed with me and said, "I don't know where it came from. It just came out." It was total nonsense, but it was totally Amy.

Amy had to return home for treatment, so she was unable to travel for the final game in the playoff series. But when I got to the stadium, someone handed me a phone message from her. It read: "Dear Dad, Chicken runs at midnight. Love, Amy."

As I was holding the note, the second baseman, Jose Lind—who spoke very little English—noticed me looking at it. "What's that?" he asked.

"Chicken runs at midnight," I answered with a chuckle.

He said, "OK." Then, as he went out onto the field, he ran around telling all the players, "Chicken runs at midnight. Chicken runs at midnight," not knowing what he was saying. Soon, in the dugout the whole team was saying, "Chicken runs at midnight. Let's go, chicken runs at midnight."

Amy was at home with her younger brother, Tim, watching the game on television when they heard one of the players yell, "Chicken runs at midnight!" They screamed and howled with laughter.

From that point on, it became an ever-present family motto. We'd start and end phone conversations with it. When a newspaper photographer laughed about my funny stance in the team picture, I told him about the "Chicken runs at midnight" phrase that inspired it. He sent me an enlarged photograph with those four words boldly printed underneath.

Those four silly words took on a meaning all their own;. they meant absolutely nothing, but to our family they came to mean everything. "Chicken runs at midnight" represented the love, the bond, the sense of humor, and the baseball we all shared. They also represented Amy, and we were losing her fast.

We lost that final baseball game and with it went my dream to go to the World Series. The loss hurt deeply. It was my last chance to share that dream with Amy. Three months later she lapsed into a coma.

I had been praying so hard for Amy to make it. I never wanted anything more in my life. Through her illness, I had regained the faith of my youth. Although many teens drift from religion, I was an oddity. Those were the years I went to daily Mass, prayed novenas and rosaries, and was even served for the bishop.

Into my twenties, religion took a backseat to baseball. By the time I was forty, I was no longer missing Mass, but God was still not the center of my life. Then, at forty-six, when Amy got her brain tumor, my world turned upside down and God ended up on top.

Sure, I pleaded and begged God to heal my little girl. But I also found the faith of my youth again. I knew that Amy would be in God's care regardless. When it came time to say goodbye, I walked in the hospital room and held her. Tears poured down my face as I hugged Amy close and thanked her. Her dream of becoming a teacher would never come to pass but she had taught me so much. Through Amy I learned about love and joy and courage—right up until the very end. Although I could never really be ready to say goodbye to my "Ames," I was ready to accept God's will.

Amy died on January 28, 1993. The family all agreed on the words for her headstone: "Chicken runs at midnight." The lady at the funeral parlor initially tried to steer us in another direction—something a little more dignified, I suppose. But it had to be "Chicken runs at midnight." To us, that phrase said it all. It kept us connected to the best of Amy.

As we planned for the funeral, I was distraught to learn Fr. David Yetsko, newly transferred to St. Maria Goretti Church in Arlington, would be saying the Mass. He had never known Amy. He had no idea how special she was. When we met for the first time to plan the Mass, I was surprised to learn Fr. David was from Pittsburgh. I quickly discovered he was a big Pirates fan, but rarely had the chance to go to any games. He did manage to make it to one game the previous season, however. It was the same one that Amy was at—the one where the "Chicken runs at midnight" motto was born.

When we realized the incredible coincidence, Fr. David held my hands and we wept together. It turned out that he was just the right priest to say the Mass. His eulogy truly captured Amy's beauty. He even managed to include "Chicken runs at midnight" in it.

Four years later, in 1997, I went south to coach the Florida Marlins. We upset the Atlanta Braves in six games to win the National League Championship. The dream I held since I was a little boy then became a reality. We were going to the World Series against the Cleveland Indians.

Although the Indians were favored to win, we held our own. After six games, the series was tied. Tim, who had just graduated from high school, was a bat boy at all six of the games. Then, for the last big game, another son, Mike, was able to take time away from college football to also put on a bat boy uniform.

The word "tense" does not describe this final face-off. In the ninth inning, the Marlins tied the score, sending the game into extra innings. In the bottom of the eleventh, with two outs, we needed just one run to win the game. Second basemen, Craig Counsell—who my kids had nicknamed "Chicken Wing" because he held his elbow up high when he batted—was on third base.

We watched breathlessly at the wind up and the pitch. It was a hit! Craig ran home and scored the winning run.

We won the World Series! The home team crowd of 67,000
fans went nuts, everyone cheering madly and jumping wildly
about.

My son, Tim, came up and ran to my arms, pointing to
the stadium clock. "Dad, look!" he screamed. "Chicken ran
at midnight!"

The large stadium clock read twelve midnight. It was Craig,
"Chicken Man," who had scored the winning run at midnight.
My adrenaline surge disappeared as if I had been zapped with
a tranquilizer dart. The crowd disappeared. I was only aware of
Mike and Tim as we held each other and bawled.

I wanted to call Amy. She knew how much the World
Series meant to me. But I knew, she was there. I could feel it.
She was there with us. Somehow, some way, that nonsensical
phrase "Chicken runs at midnight" had been a prophecy
that now connected us to her. Knowing that Amy would be
with Him, God provided us with a connection between our
two worlds during that incredible moment. The boys and I
hugged and cried and hugged and cried. No one else could
begin to understand what it all meant to the three of us.

After all the celebrating had died down at around 3
a.m., I walked back to the locker room and got my briefcase.
Opening it, I reached into a side pocket and pulled out
the phone message I always carried with me. "Dear Dad,
Chicken runs at midnight. Love, Amy."

"We did it 'Ames,'" I cried softly. "And you were with
me."

—Rich Donnelly

*Rich Donnelly is currently a coach with the Milwaukee Brewers. During the
off season, he travels around the country as a Catholic motivational speaker.
He can be contacted by calling Tiffany Rodriguez at (561) 218-5739.*

This story also appears in Amazing Grace for the Catholic Heart.

A Prayin' Man

For many men today, a "holy hour" means being able to watch the second half of a football game without interruption, and a "retreat" is a weekend that includes 36 holes of golf interspersed with appropriate beverages. In many parishes I've visited, the women far outnumber the men in the pews.

There are countless things competing for our time and attention and, frankly, we men don't always do a good job of prioritizing—of putting first things first. We're also very easily distracted; my wife has to constantly remind me to stay focused on the matter at hand. Yet men must never lose sight of the fact that bending the knee before our Heavenly Father, the source of all fatherhood (as it says in Ephesians 3:14), is job one. When men lose sight of God the Father, we lose sight of how we are to assume the vocation of father. This may happen on an individual basis or afflict an entire culture.

St. Joseph is the model for all Catholic men, especially husbands and fathers. His entire life was ordered to God. This enabled him to reflect in his actions an interior life that perfected his manhood.

We know that children learn mostly by example. They know where our hearts are and what our priorities are. One of the ways they figure this out is by how we spend our time. The quiet witness of a daily prayer life speaks volumes. There simply isn't a better example for children than a father on his knees before our Lord in prayer. This holds true as well for our spiritual fathers. The faithful are always edified and strengthened in their own prayer lives when they witness the sincere, devoted prayer of priests. Without prayer, dads and priests become less like fathers and more like mere managers.

We hear much today about absent fathers, priestless parishes, and empty seminaries. Families and parishes slog along as best they can in such circumstances, sometimes heroically, but we all know that this is far from the ideal. Fathers are irreplaceable, and calling men to fully accept the responsibilities of fatherhood is an essential element in the renewal of families and the priesthood.

The idea here isn't merely to fill a void. Instead, the presence of a father is a dynamic reality that should benefit the entire family entrusted to him. This presence presupposes a certain availability, or living for others—laying down one's life for our loved ones. This is sacrificial and thus a priestly exercise. This is how men are ordinarily called to live our Lord's enigmatic invitation to save our life by losing it.

It's no accident that the *Catechism of the Catholic Church* treats the sacraments of Matrimony and Holy Orders in the same section. These sacraments are related in that they are both directed toward the salvation of others (as seen in no. 1534). In both sacraments, though in different ways, men are empowered to participate in God's very fatherhood, which consists primarily in pouring out one's life into others.

St. Joseph was not merely present for the coming of the Savior into the world, but rather all his actions recorded in Scripture are directed to the service of the family that was entrusted to him. He teaches fathers that the key to true happiness is not in pursuing our own selfish whims, but in subordinating our time and energy—and presence—to the good of our families. We simply can't do this well unless we're men of prayer who have our priorities in order.

Maybe this weekend we'll be open to having our "holy hour" in front of the big game interrupted by those who matter most to us.

—Leon J. Suprenant, Jr.

Leon J. Suprenant, Jr. is the president of Catholics United for the Faith (CUF) and Emmaus Road Publishing, and serves as the editor-in-chief of Lay Witness *magazine, all based in Steubenville, Ohio. He is a contributor to* Catholic for a Reason III: Scripture and the Mystery of the Mass *and an adviser to Catholic Exchange's* Catholic Scripture Study (CSS). *His email address is leon@cuf.org.*

Grace from Her Fathers

Opening my front door, I was surprised to see my dad standing there. It was in the middle of the afternoon, just a few weeks before my seventh baby's due date. Although he works only a few miles away, it was not his custom to just drop by for no reason. I bluntly asked, "What happened?"

"Nothing happened, " he replied. "I just want to give you this." He held out a simple wooden rosary that he purchased when he had gone to a Marian shrine many years before. He had had it blessed, and carried it in his pocket ever since.

"You know I have rosaries," I told him.

"Just take this one," he said, "and keep it with you. Take it to the hospital when you go to have the baby and pray with it."

"OK," I said, a little annoyed that he thought my rosaries were not good enough.

"I woke up in the middle of the night," he said, "I had a strong feeling I needed to give you this rosary. I had not been thinking about you before I went to sleep. I was not dreaming. I barely slept all night. In the morning, I kept fighting the feeling, trying to talk myself out of it. By midmorning, it was overwhelming me. I had to come over and give this to you."

My annoyance turned to anxiety. I started to think, perhaps superstitiously, that my labor was doomed—or my baby was. Less than five minutes after he left—and as I stood at the window gazing at the trees in my backyard, pondering the meaning of it all —he called me on the phone. "You're supposed to wear it, I think," he said. And so, I put it around my neck and began to pray.

As my due date approached, I wore a rosary or carried one in my pocket. If I left it somewhere I began to feel naked. Fingering the beads reminded me to pray—for what I did not know. My initial anxiousness turned to calm as I obeyed my father's words and offered prayers for the unknown intention.

The day of my baby's birth initially seemed routine. By that time I was used to wearing the rosary and didn't think twice about the prayers I recited on it daily. We arrived at the hospital and labor progressed well. My husband and labor coach, David, stood at my side as I was about to give birth to our seventh child. The nurses in the room commented on my calm during the process, and the doctor joked that she was not needed since we were old pros. The nurse even called in a resident to show him how relaxing a non-medicated natural birth could be.

All calm evaporated the moment the baby was born. After two strong pushes, our baby girl slipped out. The doctor laid her on my tummy. Immediately David noticed something was wrong. "She's turning purple!" he shouted. "Theresa, she's not breathing!" The nurses rushed over and grabbed her from my tummy. She gasped for breath, and she was indeed very purple. They whisked my precious little baby away to a corner of the room, before I had a chance to stroke her cheek or whisper the name we had chosen for her.

David was shooed away when he tried to come near. Someone noticed that the baby appeared to have an obstruction in her nasal passage. They tried to intubate her nose, but kept coming upon a solid mass of some sort. "It won't go through! It won't go through!" I kept hearing. They talked amongst themselves. It was not mucous. It was not cartilage. It seemed to be bone. Two doctors tried to insert the rubber tube into her nose as well, but they couldn't. Something blocked the way.

"Maybe there is no nasal passage," someone suggested. I knew things were bad by the expressions on the doctors and nurses faces. I tried to read every expression on their faces while my body started shaking uncontrollably from the after-effect of giving birth. David and I never felt more helpless, unable to assist our child in her time of greatest need. "Please God, let it be OK," I prayed. I just kept repeating, "Please God, please."

Finally, we saw that someone was able to get a tube in her throat. As our baby flailed about and cried, she could finally get air. Babies are not mouth breathers naturally so she could have suffocated with no air had they not forced the tube and air in. Our little baby was still in distress. Monitors were quickly hooked up to her and beeped loudly to announce her struggle with every breath. Her oxygen level fell dangerously low. Her whole body would spasm as she tried to draw in air. Exams and an X-ray showed she was missing the normal hole in her nasal passage that would allow air in. This was extremely rare, we were told, and was, of course, an emergency situation. Arrangements were being considered to fly her to the nearest children's hospital for surgery to create the lacking nasal passage. She would go first; I would follow when my doctor gave the go-ahead. In the meantime, she was in the neonatal intensive care unit, going into distress on and off. If anyone touched her, her body overreacted. Her oxygen level plummeted. I longed to hold and soothe her, but I was forced to sit by and watch.

Naively, I asked the intensive care nurse, "When can I hold her?"

"You can't hold her unless she's stable!" was the curt reply. I sensed the nurse was surprised I asked.

"Is she going to be OK?" I kept asking.

No one offered any promises. Some of the replies were: "We're doing our best"; or "She's a strong one"; or "You're lucky she's so big," as she was over eight pounds. They tried to exude calm but I sensed their fear.

Fear and emptiness filled my heart at the realization that my baby might be dying. I placed my rosary in her little bassinette. David and I named her Grace Victoria—meaning grace victorious—and prayed for a miracle.

All evening, Gracie struggled in the NICU, and all evening I prayed. My brother-in-law, her uncle, Joe Pekarek, had been killed in a plane crash during my pregnancy with Grace. We had been thinking of asking him to be the baby's godfather before he was tragically killed. Now I prayed for his intercession. Could his prayers help our little Grace?

My father rushed to the hospital and blessed his little grandchild with oil. We pinned a relic of Padre Pio onto her bassinette. Dad prayed for her healing and for peace. At one moment I watched him and my husband praying together over her. Then it struck me: a circle of fathers—little Gracie's father, and grandfather, and her would-be godfather, storming heaven for a miracle for my little daughter.

Later that night when Grace's condition worsened, my husband said we should baptize her. The Catholic hospital provided the holy water and little white robe to lay over her. The nurses gave me a candle to hold and a crucifix to place by her. And so, in the darkest of nights, as the monitors bleeped and Grace struggled for breaths, her daddy poured water over her head and light shined into her soul as he baptized her in the name of the Father, and of the Son, and of the Holy Spirit. He kissed her little head and for a moment she did not go into distress. I heard a sigh, not knowing if it came from daddy or daughter.

That night, alone in my room, I prayed the "Our Father" over and over, and tried to mean every single word. "Thy kingdom come, Thy will be done."

In the morning, Gracie was still hooked up to tubes and getting oxygen, but was calmer. She was taken for a CT scan to determine the extent of her problem. The neonatalogist, two ear-nose-throat doctors, and the pediatrician were all visibly confused when they returned to us with the results.

"We don't know how to explain this," they said. The pictures were completely normal. Grace's nasal cavity was not large, but it was certainly there. The CT scan contradicted the first X-ray. They checked and rechecked everything. They ruled out any kind of mucous obstruction, or fluid, or cartilage, or bone. They had never seen anything like it. The problem had simply disappeared. When the tube was cautiously removed from my daughter, she took a deep breath and snuggled down to sleep. There was absolutely nothing wrong with her.

As strangely as this ordeal had begun, it ended. By the end of that day, I requested to nurse her. They cautioned that it was unlikely that she would or could, but she did. She eagerly nursed for fifteen full minutes. It had been excruciatingly painful to watch my daughter suffer and not be able to relieve that suffering. Now, I could care for her.

When we left the hospital, the doctors—still shaking their heads—sent us home with special tubing in case Grace had trouble breathing. They warned us that any small cold could plug up her cavity in no time and put her in trouble. Yet, this never happened.

Today, Grace is a beautiful curly-haired six year old who loves to read and play with her toy animals, or run teasingly away from her eight brothers and sisters. She has a will of steel, which I have no doubt helped her survive the first days. Gracie's story is a story of a father, grandfather, and would-be godfather's love—how prayer can literally change everything and how God the Father mercifully healed His little girl.

—Theresa Thomas

Theresa A. Thomas, a graduate of Saint Mary's College in Notre Dame, Indiana, has written for The Elkhart Truth, The National Catholic Register, Ora et Labora *online magazine, and was a story contributor for* Amazing Grace for Mothers. *She is a regular contributor and columnist for* Today's Catholic, *the official newspaper of the Diocese of Fort Wayne–South Bend. She, her husband, David, and their nine children, ages one to eighteen, reside in northern Indiana, where she spends her days building pyramids out of clay, supervising bird reports, and drawing math problems on a whiteboard as a home-schooling mom.*

Is Eight Enough?

Remember the television show *Eight is Enough?* My wife, Patti, and I had enjoyed that show back in the 70s. By the 90s, we had eight children of our own. We thought it was enough.

Then our friend, Evan, paid us a visit. He came through town on sabbatical from his work as a missionary in Kisii, Kenya. We were expecting just to have dinner with him, but he was hoping for something more.

"Is there anything we could do for you?" I asked. I was thinking along the lines of a small donation or occasionally sending packages of goodies not available to him in Kenya.

A sly grin passed over his face. "Well," he began, "I have a bright young student who desperately wants to go to school in the United States. Would you consider taking him in?"

While Patti and I were recovering from the shock of being asked to take in a boy rather than send money or beef jerky, Evan elaborated.

"Calvin is a very good boy. His parents both died of AIDS and he was living with his two brothers. I found out he often went hungry and walked an hour and a half each way to school." Evan took a breath. He had our attention so he continued. "I invited him to stay at the school with me during the week so he can eat properly. He wanted me to bring him home with me, but I am seventy now so that would be impossible. I've been asking around in Bismarck to see if there is a family who might be willing to take Calvin into their home."

Calvin had our sympathy, but we already had eight children ranging from a one-year-old to a 19-year-old in college: six boys and two girls. "Even if we wanted to," Patti ventured, "we cannot afford one more."

Evan shrugged. "I know. That's why I was not planning to ask you. But after a few families suggested you, I thought I had to at least bring it up. One person thought that since you had so many kids already, maybe one more would not make much of a difference!'" Patti and I looked at each other and smiled.

Then, Evan suddenly brightened. "What if I got a family or two to help with the expenses?"

I loved being a father. So much of life was merely passing, but children were forever. It had always felt like an honor to me to be entrusted with God's little ones. The idea of becoming a father to an orphan intrigued me. I looked at Patti again. We knew each other well enough to know that the door to our hearts had opened just a crack.

In reality, no one really believed that Calvin would actually get permission to leave the country. At fifteen, he had no birth certificate. Before Evan left Bismarck, he had two families willing to help support Calvin and our promise to at least pray about it. Somehow we never actually got around to giving a bonafide "yes." When Evan emailed us that Calvin had successfully gotten a birth certificate, the wheels were set in motion. But there were still a lot of hoops to jump through. Terrorists had recently blown up the U.S. embassy in Nairobi, so getting a passport and U.S. visa for an orphan to travel here would not be easy. Everyone on all sides prayed, and with the help of North Dakota's U.S. congressman, Calvin joined us in July of 2002. He easily became a part of our family. Our son, Tyler—who is a month younger—quickly became best buddies with Calvin, calling him "his brother from the other color mother."

We thought we were being good Christians to take Calvin in, but when we heard the rest of the story, we realized it was we who had been blessed. God had chosen us to answer a special prayer that bordered on the miraculous.

Years earlier, Calvin gently closed his paperback novel as he lay in his mud hut. It was getting dark in the one-room home he shared with his two brothers. There was no money for oil to burn in their kerosene lantern, so reading needed to stop at sunset.

Ignoring the rumbling coming from his empty stomach, Calvin thought about the main character in his novel: a boy who left Africa to live with relatives in the United States and go to school there. "Maybe I could go there someday," Calvin dreamed.

"Dear God," he began praying, "Please let me go to school in the United States one day." Although it seemed that God had not answered so many of his prayers before, Calvin prayed with the trust of a child. At thirteen, his childhood seemed to have been lost long ago. Both his parents had died of AIDS, leaving Rogers, fifteen, Calvin, eleven, and Joash, nine, among Kenya's 650,000 AIDS orphans. The boys had loved their parents deeply. The ache caused by their absence overshadowed each day.

Relatives helped out a little, but as time went on, the assistance was gradually withdrawn. An uncle continued to pay the fees for him to attend school, but it was a long walk for Calvin from his hut to St. Patrick's Elementary School. Since he rarely had dinner the night before, his feet felt heavy as he trudged along. "If only I could go to school in the United States," Calvin began thinking on these long walks. And again, he would pray.

When Calvin revealed his prayer to his older brother and an aunt, they laughed at him. "You only own two pairs of pants and have no money," his aunt had said. "How do you think you are going to get to the United States?"

Rogers was sympathetic but no more encouraging. "Why don't you pray for something more practical, like a bigger garden?" he had asked. The boys' only reliable source of food was a garden. It was not very big, but it provided vegetables in addition to occasional donations of food from others.

Then, Evan Beauchamp came to work at the school as a missionary for the diocese of Bismarck, North Dakota. When he noticed that Calvin had a sore on his foot for several weeks that was not healing, he knew it must be the effects of malnutrition. He learned of the boy's hardships and invited Calvin to live with him during the school week and then return to help his brothers on the weekends. Calvin overflowed with appreciation. Not only would he receive better nutrition, but perhaps God was answering his prayer to eventually go to school in the United States.

It was not long before Calvin asked if perhaps Evan could take him back to the United States with him one day. Evan told him that would never be possible. Calvin smiled as if he understood, but he kept praying and he kept asking. Finally, Evan told Calvin he would ask his friends when he returned to the United States for his mid-service sabbatical the next year.

It was a month after Calvin joined us that we learned of his prayer. We were truly in awe at such faithfulness and at the realization that God had picked our family to answer a young boy's prayers. Calvin is a much-loved member of our household. He and Tyler both graduated from high school with honors this year. Calvin was awarded a four-year scholarship to attend the University of Mary. He is determined to return to Kenya after graduation to help his countrymen in whatever way God leads him. It has been an honor to have Calvin call me "Dad."

So, after Calvin joined our family, was nine finally enough? Well, we honestly thought so. Then, Evan hoped to have Calvin's younger brother, Joash, also come to school here. Again, he sheepishly asked us and again we said no ... at first. After a lot of praying, we changed our minds and decided there was room for one more. Joash just finished his freshman year and is doing well. There are no more little brothers at home, so maybe ten is enough now. We'll see.

—Mark Armstrong

Mark Armstrong is a co-editor of Amazing Grace for Fathers. *His biography appears at the end of the book.*

Through the Eyes of Grace

We were celebrating my son's eleventh birthday when the phone call came. Time froze as still as the cold February day when the voice on the phone told me that my father had passed away. A heart attack, I was told. My heart fell along with my tears at the realization that there was no more time now. *Oh Lord,* I thought, *I really could have used a little more time.*

My father, Bill Velline, and I never had the chance to get close. My parents had had a bitter divorce when I was eight and my brother, Matt, was four. Our mother's resentment certainly contributed to the distance my brother and I both felt from our father. But as the years passed, we realized there was more than just mileage between us; there was also an emotional distance. Dad had conquered his alcoholism, but he still struggled with manic depression, which added to the problem.

He had tried to be involved in our lives after the divorce by reaching out in little ways. Although my dad was neither religious nor Catholic, he gave me a book that awakened my faith and led me to join the Catholic Church in 1995. During my youth, we had been nominal Lutherans. After the divorce, church went by the wayside. One day when I was visiting Dad at his cramped, disheveled apartment, I told him that I had started praying the rosary. Strangely, he got up in search of something and returned with a Miraculous Medal. Then, Dad related the story of how a friend of his had been at an old abandoned mission site in northern North Dakota with a metal detector and found this medal in the soil. "You have to have this," he said. "I've been saving it for ten years and I never knew why." He also gave me a rosary blessed by Pope John Paul II from a dear friend of his who had been involved in the pro-life movement.

During one visit, less than a year before my father's death, he seemed particularly depressed. He once used to sketch beautiful pictures for me, so, I had brought along some colored pencils and a sketch pad as a small gift. I thought, in some little way, it might be an avenue to bring some joy back into his life. Before leaving, I looked searchingly into his dispirited eyes and saw that there was nothing more that he could give. "I'll see you later," I said with a heavy heart. On the drive home, I prayed to God for understanding and compassion. I begged Him to help me see my dad through different eyes. I decided to pray the sorrowful mysteries of the Rosary. When I got to Jesus carrying the cross, it was as if a veil had suddenly been lifted. I was given a vision of Jesus struggling on the road to Calvary. As the vision became clearer, it was not the Lord's face I saw, but that of my own father. I could see how painstakingly he was carrying the weight of his cross. At that point my heart was given the grace to see my dad in the precious way that God loves him. I could see the gentle, wounded man who was just trying to make his way. "Lord, please," I cried, "Just hold him in the palm of your hand."

Several months later, my dad came to visit me. At the time, I did not feel it was a very good visit. Dad was slipping into a deep depression and struggling with personal problems. Before we parted, I was uncharacteristically stern with him. "Dad, you have to take God's hand and let Him help you," I pleaded. "You will one day stand before God and discover all the times He wanted to help you out of the darkness. At least find a pastor and talk to him." During a later conversation, which turned out to be our last, I learned he had done just that. It was my only relief when a week later he had died unexpectedly of a heart attack.

Not expecting many people at the funeral, my brother and I decided to hold the service at the funeral home. There had been a time when my father was vibrant and outgoing and even famous, but that had been long ago. In his younger years, he and his brother Bobby—Bobby Vee—played together in Bobby Vee and the Shadows. I was surprised and touched when a local radio station played their music the whole day of the funeral, dedicated in the memory of Dad. Dick Clark, the Shirelles, and other famous groups of that era even sent flowers to the funeral home.

Uncle Bob had asked if I would say something at the funeral. I wanted to pay tribute to my dad and express my love for him, and yet, because of our complicated relationship, I had no idea what to say. I prayed for guidance. As I sat down to write, the memory of my vision of Dad carrying the cross came flooding back to my mind and filled me with love and understanding. I picked up a pen. Twenty minutes later, the poem I would share at the funeral the next day was complete.

When Matt and I arrived for the funeral, we were shocked when we entered the room and found it overflowing with people. We heard story after story of how our father had touched their lives. There was an outpouring of tenderness and affection as many got up to share how much our father meant to them. Matt and I were taken aback. How could we have known so little about our father while others knew so much? Why was it so difficult for Dad to have a close relationship with us when he had shared so freely with strangers?

I had thought and prayed for him often, and sometimes grieved over the relationship we had missed. And yet, on the day of his funeral, I met my father anew. Then, eight years later, God brought my father even closer to me. At that time, my husband and I owned and operated a Catholic bookstore. One day, an advertising salesman came in. During the course of our conversation, it came up that he would soon be attending a reunion in Fargo where my dad and uncle had grown up. He seemed to be about their age, so I asked if he knew Uncle Bob. We discovered that his cousin had been my father's best friend, Jim. Once the salesman realized that I was Bill Velline's daughter, he began sharing stories of their young adult years together. He came to the store again shortly after and brought old photographs of him and my father. I was in awe. Only God could have arranged such a meeting and opportunity for me to feel closer to my dad.

In the years since my father's death, I have come to recognize that God gives gifts in the most unexpected and unusual ways. I could not have known on the day Dad died that God would continue to reveal my father to me in ways that couldn't be accomplished while he was still here. It is through the memories that are so kindly shared by others that I have come to understand who my father truly was. I realize now that I have not only this lifetime but all of eternity to get to know him fully. The love I have for my father has grown since his death. God has delivered me from all feelings of bitterness or abandonment. The Lord now allows me to see Dad not through my own eyes, but through eyes of grace.

"Through His Eyes"

He sat before me silently,
Lost within his thoughts.
I struggled, as I often did,

To find the key to fit the lock
To the door that led to that secret place
Deep within his heart
Where hope and joy and dreams still lived,
Of which I yearned to be a part.

But, alas, the key it did not fit
Like the thousand times before,
And so we sat and just simply were;
Both wanting so much more.

As the moments quietly slipped away
In the silence of that night,
I reached to gently clasp his hand
And tell him it was all right.

As I rose to say good-bye to him,
And I bent to kiss his cheek,
I gazed into those gentle eyes
And I prayed for just one peek.
Just a glimpse, I asked of God
To see him as You do.

And then a gentle voice said, "Come, I have a gift for you."
And at that moment His hand drew back the veil from my eyes,
And I got to glimpse that precious soul that dwelt so deep inside.
"This is MY beloved child," said that gentle voice so clear,
"And I love him more than you'll ever know
So do not have such fear.

One day soon I'll come for him
And I'll bind up all his wounds
And then this precious soul will soar

As I always meant him to."
That moment I will cherish
Until I, too, draw my last breath.

And then we'll be united in this mystery called death.
I'll gaze into those gentle eyes of a soul that I now know.
I'll tell him then as I do now
Dad, I love you so.

—Christene Bartels

Christene Bartels lives near Fisher, Minnesota, with her husband Steve and their three children, Nick (20), Joey (15), and Isaiah (6). Christene entered into full communion with the Catholic Church on May 28, 1995. Her children soon followed, and Steve joined them in December of 1999. In 1995, on the feast of St. Joseph, Christene and Steve opened St. Joseph's Catholic Gift and Book Store in Grand Forks, North Dakota to help others know and love their faith.

Chapter 4

A Father's Humor

They're Driving Me Crazy

You shouldn't drive when you're under the influence. Of course, I'm talking about the influence of children.

I remember taking my driver's license test when I was sixteen. I was nervous, but the test wasn't too difficult. I passed without a problem, which meant I was certified to handle a vehicle in a controlled environment—sans children. Twenty years later, I was introduced to a new type of driving—one in which you attempt to concentrate on the traffic while your seat is being kicked by a three-year-old who's singing "Old MacDonald Had a Farm" at the top of her lungs and pelting you with Cheerios. They never mentioned that in driver education class. I've petitioned the federal government to require that all children have a warning label sewn onto their shirts. It will read, "Do not operate heavy machinery if this child is in the same vehicle with you."

But I throw caution to the wind and routinely operate heavy machinery with four children —ages four months to nine years—sitting behind me in our mini-van. A recent trip to the grocery store will illustrate this experience.

"Dad, I found half a cheeseburger under my seat. Can I eat it? I took the lint off it already."

"Dad, Maria's looking at me! Tell her to stop it!"

"Dad, would you turn on the music? ... not that CD, the other one ... not that song, number twelve ... turn it up, I can't hear it ..."

"Can I open a window? ... But, Dad, I can't breathe in here ... what do you mean all my talking is sucking all the air out of the car? ..."

I usually suggest that my kids bring a book in the car to keep themselves quietly entertained. My philosophy is if they won't allow it through airport security, I don't want it in my car either. The kids ignore my advice and smuggle contraband items into the van.

"Dad, I can't get the test tubes from my chemistry set to stay in the cup holder. They keep falling out ... what do you mean I shouldn't have brought them in the car? ... you never want me to use them in the house because they're too messy."

I make a mental note to hose out the car later in the day. One time I found a clump of radishes growing underneath a seat. It was a discarded school science experiment. You wouldn't think radishes could grow like that under a seat. I think they had been watered with spilt juice boxes and fertilized with cookie crumbs.

"Dad, Maria won't look at me any more but I want her to!"

"Hey Dad, guess what? I found some french fries to go with the cheeseburger ... Maria, stop grabbing my fries!"

I glanced in the rearview mirror. It looked like the Battle of Gettysburg if it had been fought with stale french fries. The carnage was gruesome. But it may have just been ketchup stains.

Then I backed the car out of the garage. Next time I'm taking the bus.

—Tim Bete

Tim Bete's column has been featured in the Christian Science Monitor *and more than a dozen parenting magazines. His column has also appeared on CatholicExchange.com, ParentingHumor.com, CatholicMom.com, and iParenting.com.*

Have Basement, Will Accumulate

Basements didn't mean much to me when my wife and I were first married. Back then, I was young and carefree. What did I know?

But it wasn't long before heredity kicked in and it dawned on me that a basement holds an amazing potential for storing vast amounts of worthless junk. Lauren and I have been married almost fifteen years now, and a broken toilet recently showed me how far I've come. I fixed the plumbing problem with a rubber contraption called a Bullseye flapper. The scary part was, I not only knew what that was, I actually had one right there in the basement.

Before I was married, if you had asked me for a Bullseye flapper I'd have referred you to the nearest pasture. So when, and why, did I start hoarding Bullseye flappers? And why does my basement look more and more like the markdown room at Lloyd's House of Junk? After consulting with several married friends and studying my family history, I've determined this is a process most men go through: we grow up, we get married, and we gradually begin stocking our basements with miscellaneous bits and pieces of every house we've ever lived in.

Here's a sampling of what's sitting in my basement right now. Screws from outlet covers I've replaced over the years. Countless lumber scraps, none large enough to be really useful. Rubber gaskets from a car I owned in high school. Leftover wire ranging in size from miniature (three inches long) to jumbo (four inches long).

This behavior is not my fault. It's inherited. When it comes to saving worthless junk, my dad is the reigning

national champion. I think it's because his father once owned
a hardware store and he's trying to carry on the tradition.
Dad's shed is stocked with old, dirty lumber scraps, warped
lawn mower wheels and coffee cans full of rusty nuts and
bolts. But the really good stuff, the junk that can't be exposed
to the elements, fills the basement.

Last winter, Mom cleaned the basement, putting
roughly half of Dad's junk into a large barrel earmarked for
the garbage truck. Into that barrel, if you can believe this,
she threw some items just because they were dirt-encrusted
and hadn't been touched since the Ford Administration.
Corroded faucets with no handles. Assorted moldy boots.
Pieces of broken pencils. Paint brushes with bristles so stiff
they could be used as hammers.

Then Dad came downstairs. He saw the junk barrel
and started pawing through it to retrieve things Mom really
should have saved, such as broken chunks of bathroom tile.
Mom threatened him bodily harm if he touched one rusty
bolt.

Back one more generation, my grandmother carried
the pack-rat gene. She recently gave me some stuff that
had gathered dust in her basement workshop for twenty-
five years. Included was a sixteen-drawer box stocked with
treasures from another generation: broken jigsaw blades, a
tube of glue from 1966, and a small box labeled "japanned
tubular rivets."

All of these things make a great addition to my basement
collection. After it ages a few more years, it'll be ready for
a garage sale—an important part of the junk saver's life.
I think we love garage sales because they confirm in our
minds that our own junk has value. We peruse another guy's
treasure, then give him money for it. Often this involves a
filthy, decades-old electrical appliance that the seller assures

you "works just fine." To prove it, he has priced it at twenty-five cents. You get it home and find that it does indeed "work fine"—as a doorstop.

But you've paid good money for this thing and you're not throwing it away. You take it apart to have a look, forget how it goes back together and end up keeping it, in pieces, on a basement shelf. Hey, you might need the parts someday.

Maybe the reason pack rats have so many tiny, unrelated bits of junk is that we love to take things apart. In my basement sits the skeleton of a Eureka vacuum cleaner that I tried to fix two years ago. I took the whole thing apart, cleaned it, put it back together and plugged it in. It sounded like a 747 trying to take off while dragging a pregnant moose. Maybe the problem had something to do with the leftover pieces that were piled on the workbench. My wife, a nonadventurous type, went out and bought a new one.

Meanwhile, I held onto what was left of the old Eureka. This despite the fact I have no idea how to fix a vacuum cleaner. But my junk-saving relatives would be proud. Together, we've probably amassed enough worthless items to build something potentially dangerous, then sell it at a garage sale to some poor sap who'll take it apart and store the pieces in his basement—on the shelf, right next to his Bullseye flapper.

—Jim Killam

Jim Killam is a free-lance writer and teaches journalism at Northern Illinois University. He is co-author of When God is the Life of the Party *(NavPress, 2003) and* Rescuing the Raggedy Man *(Xulon Press, 2004). He and his wife, Lauren, have three teenagers.*

Breaking the Cycle

It wasn't meant as an insult. It just came out that way. My daughter had just finished cleaning her bedroom. Her menagerie of stuffed animals was now securely confined to one area. Her pile of favorite books sat neatly on the proper shelves rather than all over the floor. The freshly laundered clothes were off her desk and packed away in her dresser drawers.

I walked into her room and the unusual cleanliness took my breath away. That's when I said,

"I didn't know you had carpeting in here!"

We could finally see the carpet in her room. My daughter didn't laugh. She took the room cleaning seriously, although not seriously enough to clean more often.

"Very funny!" she said sarcastically, as the scent of Lemon Pledge floated through the room, and as a stuffed bunny rabbit threatened to topple from the pile onto the floor. I shattered her pride. Bad move.

This is an age-old battle, I just know it—kids and their parents arguing over messy rooms. I am sure that back in the time of the cave dwellers the cave mothers were yelling at their cave children: "Why can't you pick up your rocks and bones when I tell you to? And why are your loincloths always in a wrinkled pile in the corner just minutes after I got done beating them against the river rocks? Just for that, you can't help your father try to invent fire again tonight!"

Messy rooms. I did it. You did it. We all did it. We all kept our rooms as clean as horse stalls on an abandoned farm.

My oldest son just got finished writing an important research paper for school. Before starting the project, he needed a lot of reference material. He went to the library and came home with a tall stack of books. The paper was finished weeks and weeks ago. The books are still on his floor, and on his desk, and on his bed. (I think he has carpeting, too!)

In the meantime, our youngest son has apparently developed an allergy—to clothes hangers. I think he presumes the floor works just fine. He must also have an aversion to his dresser drawers, preferring to place piles of freshly and neatly folded laundry on his desk or under his bed. My wife may go insane.

Of course, as I sit here casting aspersions, a potential avalanche of papers sits unsteadily on my desk. If I type too hard on the keyboard the papers will fall. One false move and a landslide will bury the mound of papers that covers the carpeting that I know is there.

There seems to be a pattern here that must be generational. The best that I can do might be to wait them out. Once they move away to college, I can start filling their rooms—and their floors—with my stuff.

—Tim Herrera

Tim Herrera is a nationally-recognized family writer, humorist, public speaker, and father of four teenagers. He is the author of three published collections of warm and amusing family essays. His work has been featured in dozens of publications including the New York Times Syndicate, Parenting Humor, *and* The Family Digest. *Tim is the author of* From Wedgies to Feeding Frenzies: A Semi-Survival Guide for Parents of Teens. *To learn more, visit www.timherrera.com.*

Fairweather Fans

"Remember, Coach Taylor, we parents are
100% behind you, win or tie."

When "Mommy Only" Leaves Daddy Lonely

Think about the most spirit-crushing rejection you ever got from a girl—maybe the one who said, "No way; but your best friend's really cute!" That's just a warm-up for the ego blow you feel when you, instead of your wife, pick up your child for bed and he wails like you're the monster of his nightmares. This was no fun for my wife, either, because occasionally she likes to feel that she's not still physically attached to every child to whom she has given birth.

We told ourselves that children routinely go through favoritism stages of playing, eating, or reading with only Mom or Dad. Heck, Oedipus even killed his father and married his mother. So in a way, I was lucky. But his father had abandoned him on a mountain, and I hadn't even left my son in the yard. I had to ask Alec why only Mommy could put him to bed.

"I like the way she looks," he explained.

I couldn't argue with that, but I knew this really wasn't about his mom's long dark hair.

Thinking that this was actually a natural result of my wife spending more time with our son, I started looking for things to do with him like taking him on errands, riding bikes, making his breakfast and lunch on weekends, and initiating games. When he chose an inopportune time to say, "Daddy, will you draw with me?" I shut off the computer and picked up crayons.

Meanwhile, my wife told Alec it would help her if we traded nights; she'd put him to bed one night, me the next. He agreed but quickly developed selective amnesia, insisting it was her turn six nights in a row.

On one of these nights I probed to find out what he liked about "the way mommy looks." He said, "I like her slippers." Geez, was that all? Regina kicked off her green plaid slippers; I stuffed in my feet and sat on the floor next to Alec's bed. I felt a little funny, but Alec giggled and went to sleep. Voila!

Ah, but men are fickle at this age. After two nights, the slippers had lost their magic. He announced, "I like her robe."

Now, I think of myself as a pretty open-minded guy. Milton Berle and Max Klinger from *M.A.S.H.* wore women's clothes, and no one doubted their masculinity. Of course, they had two things going for them: They smoked cigars and they were ugly, but who's noticing.

I threw the robe over my shoulders and sat on the floor, telling myself, "There is nothing wrong with wearing my wife's robe in the interest of my son." Alec went to sleep, but I wondered if he was some sort of gifted prankster.

Fortunately, he made no more wardrobe demands. And possessing a child's sense of fair play, he responded well to another strategy: We told him that each night one of us would read him a book, and the other would put him to bed. When he chose my wife to read, he accepted the downside of the deal—me carrying him to bed.

After two months of these varied tactics, Alec was happy with either of us tucking him in. In fact, he seems to have developed a preference for me even without the robe and green slippers. I've offered my wife my leather slippers.

—Patrick Boyle

Patrick Boyle's column, "A Father's Place," appears in the Gazette newspaper chain based in Montgomery County, Maryland. He is editor of Youth Today, *a Washington, D.C.-based newspaper for people who work with kids, and has written about child and family issues for* Child, Parenting, *the* Baltimore Sun, *and* Newsday, *among others. Boyle is a veteran journalist who has served as a reporter on several dailies, has won a dozen journalism awards, and has published a book,* Scout's Honor, *which explores how child molesters operate in Boy Scout troops. He lives in Maryland with his wife and two children. Patrick can be reached at PatrickBoyle1@cs.com.*

A Man's Guide to the Delivery Room

My wife and I recently had our fourth child. I've been with my wife during the deliveries of all of our children. Nothing can prepare you for the event.

You can attend childbirth classes and read books but, for some unknown reason, they always focus on the woman having the baby. So, as a public service to future fathers everywhere, I will answer the most common questions men have about what really happens in the delivery room.

What is the most painful part of labor?

Please sit down before reading any further. The following statement is extremely graphic and may shock you.

When your wife is in the hospital, the TV remote control will be attached to her bed. You may have to go for up to twenty-four hours with a remote in the room that you cannot touch.

I know many men reading this column are breaking into a cold sweat. Some are weeping. That's OK. Let it out.

Why is the remote control attached to the bed?

No one knows. We just have to accept that it is the way God created the bed and be thankful that there is a remote control at all. Because you are used to watching television at the speed of eighty-five channels per minute, labor will be a real test for you.

Can the remote control be surgically removed from the bed? I really need to hold it.

No. Insurance companies no longer cover this procedure because they consider it "elective surgery." This is only one of the major problems with the health care system in this country.

How bad will the pain be?

You will experience contractions in your hand because you're used to holding a remote at all times. The contractions will start about twenty minutes apart but will soon progress to two to three minutes apart. The pain will become unbearable when your wife is watching *Oprah* and *Sports Center* is about to come on.

I don't think I can endure that level of pain. What can I do to get through it?

First, try to relax. Move around if it makes you more comfortable. Experiment with different positions. Get on your hands and knees and rock back and forth. Try squatting or lie on your side. Some men find taking a warm bath helps.

Take deep breaths. Moan if you feel like it. If your mouth gets dry, eat some ice chips.

Focus on an object other than the remote. Having a photograph of your home theatre system can be reassuring. Remember that you will soon be going home and you will be able to hold your universal remote for hours at a time—especially when you're rocking your new baby at two a.m.

If the pain gets too great, ask the doctor for some medication. A little Nubain (a drug similar to morphine in strength) can really take the edge off the pain of that tethered remote.

One last tip: If your new child is a boy, while still in the delivery room, call "dibs for life" on your home TV remote control. Within three years he'll be fighting you for it.

—Tim Bete

Tim Bete is the author of several stories in this book. His biography appears after "They're Driving Me Crazy," the first story of this chapter.

The Children of Israel

"Dad," announced little Joey, "there's something I can't figure out."

"What's that, Joey?" his father asked him.

"Well, according to the Bible, the children of Israel crossed the Red Sea, right?"

"Right."

"And the children of Israel beat up the Philistines, right?"

"Er, right."

"And the children of Israel built the Temple, right?"

"Again, you're right."

"And the children of Israel fought the Egyptians, and the children of Israel fought the Romans, and the children of Israel were always doing something important, right?"

"All that is right, too," agreed Joey's dad, "So what's your question?"

"What were all the grown-ups doing?"

Wanted: Father

Job description:

Long-term (i.e., lifetime) position in challenging and ever-changing work environment. Candidates must possess excellent communication skills and be willing to adopt a G-rated vocabulary. Applicants must also trade in any existing sports vehicles for a "babe"-repelling, baby-friendly minivan.

Some undercover work necessary such as checking up on kids and getting to the bottom of who ate the rest of the cookies hidden on the top shelf behind the canned goods. Job entails challenging, exciting work with occasional elements of repetition and monotony. (For instance, playing Candyland 1,000 times, teaching the "ABCs," and repeating *ad nauseum* "Remember to turn off the lights.")

Qualifications:

Unconditional love. Even after being told "You don't know anything."

Infinite patience. Especially after a long day's work when asked to start a barbecue, fix broken bikes and toys, untangle fishing lines twelve times in one hour, and enough energy left over to read "Go Dog Go" for the 117th time.

Humility. Essential for all the times you will hear "That's not the way Mommy does it."

Strong skills in negotiation, conflict resolution, and crisis management. Having the wisdom of Solomon is a plus.

Keen organization skills. Necessary to separate kids' artwork and toys from junk mail, garbage, and science projects.

Accounting skills. Must balance petty cash disbursements and outgoing products in an equitable manner to avoid hearing "He got more than me!"

Salesmanship. Must be able to sell kids on why the $20 pair of shoes is actually much better than the $80 pair. Job also entails door-to-door selling of raffle tickets and cookies as you become known as "Mr. Fundraiser."

Physical requirements:
Very thick skin. Willingness to be hated until teen needs $5 or permission to go somewhere.

Physical endurance. Stamina to push swings until your arms feel like they will fall off. Legs must be strong enough to climb up snowy hills while pulling a full sled. You must also posses "faster-than-a-speeding bullet" speed, in case the screams coming from the backyard are ever an actual emergency.

Height and looks unimportant. Regardless of your actual appearance, your children will be so convinced that you are the tallest, strongest dad in the neighborhood that they will actually challenge other kids' fathers to fights. Be ready.

Travel requirements:
Late night trips to the emergency room essential— usually for ear infections that didn't seem so critical during daylight hours. Also, will be called on for occasional carpooling. Travel may include overnight camping trips to mosquito-infested Scout camps and an infinite number of sporting events beginning with Pee Wee-something or other. No reimbursement for mileage or expenses incurred.

Technical experience:
Broad base of knowledge helpful so you need not make up answers to questions such as: "Why do you have hair

growing out of your ears?" and "Why is our cat having babies?" Additional expertise will be learned later from Chinese product instruction sheets explaining how to assemble cheap and very breakable toys. This will prepare you for the challenge of one day figuring out hand-held video games, kids' computer programs, and Ipods.

Language requirements:

Understanding and speaking baby talk fluently. As child progresses, parenting classes available for learning teen jargon and for screening music and movies for appropriateness.

Career advancement opportunities:

None. You begin at the pinnacle of your career. During the teen years, you will actually be demoted. By the time you are a grandfather, you will be able to climb back up on your pedestal.

Salary:

Not enough to buy all the cool stuff that all the other kids have.

Benefits:

Boundless opportunities for spiritual growth, lifetime supply of hugs, and the indescribable joy of grandchildren.

—Mark Armstrong

Mark Armstrong is a co-editor of Amazing Grace for Fathers. *His biography appears at the end of the book.*

A Biased "Priest"

Looking over at my wife, I motioned to her that I would take our energetic four-year-old out of the main body of the Church. James was not really being bad—but with an all-boy crew of five, we did not always make it to the closing song still sitting in the pew as one unit.

Mass was almost over, so I escorted James into one of the rooms near the church vestibule. It just so happened that a make-shift confessional had been set up in anticipation of a parish penance service. Seeing this, James went behind the screen to "be the priest" and wanted me to confess to him. Pleased at my son's interest in taking the role of priest, I played along.

"Well," I began, "I should try to pray more; and sometimes, I'm not as nice to Mommy as I should be. I should help around the house more." I came up with a few other general things and then waited for James' response.

Lowering his voice with an air of authority, he doled out a litany of penances. "You need to help with the dishes more and be nicer to Mommy and pray more prayers and, and...." Then, James paused for just a moment before he handed down what he surely viewed as the most important penance. "And, you're not allowed to give spanks to James anymore."

A self-serving penance if ever I heard one.

—Matthew Pinto

Matthew Pinto is the co-creator and an editor of the Amazing Grace *series. His biography appears at the end of the book.*

Teed Off Dad

"Great, Dad—a couple more rounds
of golf and my sand box will be filled."

The Shoes of a Red Sox Fan

If you want to know how a person feels, you need to walk a mile in his or her shoes. If you want to know what it's like to be a Boston Red Sox fan, try walking a mile in my son's sneakers.

My six-year-old son, Paul, named his gym shoes after Red Sox players—one current, one former. Paul named his left sneaker "No" after Nomar Garciaparra. He named his right sneaker "Mo" after former Red Sox slugger Mo Vaughn.

Paul's sneakers might have been named after Cincinnati Reds players, but I convinced him otherwise. I grew up in Massachusetts and have been a Red Sox fan my entire life. When I was thirteen, my dad took me to the seventh game of the 1975 World Series against the Cincinnati Reds. The Reds won and I was crushed.

Fourteen years later, I married a Reds fan and moved to Ohio, proving love is stronger than baseball. But when Paul expressed an interest in becoming a Reds fan, I had to intercede and show him there was another option—an option where pitchers aren't forced to hit and a life of tireless hope and unfulfilled dreams awaits. I told him about the American League and the Boston Red Sox.

Each morning during the regular season, Paul followed the same ritual. He got up, ran downstairs and tore open the sports page. He poured over the Red Sox box score, reviewing the day's starting pitchers and memorizing as many stats his six-year-old brain could hold. Then, he put on "No" and "Mo" and got on with the business of the day.

While driving Paul to a tee-ball game during the summer, I had a talk with him about being a good sport and the importance of enjoying the game regardless of whether you win or lose.

"If you only enjoy playing baseball when you win, you may have a lot of unhappy seasons," I told him.

"You mean like the Detroit Tigers?" he questioned. "They're on pace to lose 120 games and beat the 1962 New York Mets record for most loses in a season."

I'd been thinking about his tee-ball team, but my advice was a good thing for the Tigers to remember, too.

Paul was gleeful as the Red Sox won game after game during the regular season. As the playoffs approached, I knew we should hope for the best while bracing for the worst. I remembered my dad's words after the Red Sox's devastating loss in the seventh game of the 1975 World Series. "We'll get 'em next year," he said.

But, we didn't get 'em the next year or the year after that. And, after moving to Ohio, I stopped following the Red Sox quite as closely—until Paul took an interest in them.

Paul and I commiserated when the New York Yankees finished off Boston in game seven of the American League Championship Series, ending our dream of a Red Sox World Series victory.

"We'll get 'em next year," I said—words that came partly because I believed them and partly because I wanted Paul to know what to tell his son when the Red Sox lost.

"I think you're right, Dad," Paul said. "The Red Sox will win next year!"

Paul's newfound love for the Red Sox and unshakable faith in the future make me proud. So much so, I've adopted a new morning ritual. As I get ready for work, I put on my brown dress shoes, which I have named "No" and "Mo."

If I'm going to continue to be a Red Sox fan, I want to walk in the hope-filled shoes of a six-year-old boy.

—Tim Bete

Tim Bete is the author of several stories in this book. His biography appears after "They're Driving Me Crazy," the first story of this chapter.

Putting Out a Call

It happens in my house maybe fifty times a day, whenever the phone rings.

"The phone's ringing! Where's the phone?" I yell.

"I don't know," one of the boys yells without even looking away from the Gamecube. "You had it last," he points to little sister.

"I had it, then I gave it to you," she accuses another brother.

The phone rings the second time. The cordless receiver is MIA ... again.

"You had it in your room, didn't you?" I ask the middle son.

Then comes the third ring. Still no phone.

"I put it back and then he took it." He points to his younger brother, like a dramatic witness identifying a defendant at trial.

Finally, the fourth ring triggers the answering machine: "Hi, you've reached the Herreras..."

Callers always reach our house, but don't always reach the people living there. We're always scrambling to find the phone. Instead of being in the base recharger, the phone is between couch cushions, on the floor, inside shoes, or in one of the kids' bedrooms. The glory of the cordless phones ushered in the age of misplaced receivers.

My wife and I thought we solved the phone problem a few months ago when we bought a certain high-tech gizmo. This not-so-cheap model came with one base and *three* phones. That was the solution ... three phones! Not two, but three! Our problems would be solved. We got home and I immediately installed the base in the kitchen, put one phone in the master bedroom and the third in the garage. Putting an extension in the garage was a stroke of genius, I figured. The boys are always in there lifting weights, playing ping-pong or hiding from chores.

Yes, three phones with an extension in the garage was the answer to our phone shortage ... *not!* It seems that having three cordless phones now means we have three phones to lose at any one time.

The phones end up in all kinds of weird places, but not one of our four children is ever guilty of misplacing them. Apparently, someone sneaks in and callously scatters phones throughout our house. It must be the same person who tosses shoes and socks on the carpet like confetti during a victory parade.

The only real solution is to return to the good old days when houses had only one black, ten pound phone that had an industrial cable connecting the receiver to the base. The kind of phone your grandmother had. The kind of phone you would never, ever find in someone's sock drawer.

I should consult my sister about this. She has saved just about everything from our younger days. I'll call her and ask as soon as I can find a phone.

—Tim Herrera

Tim Herrera is the author of several stories in this book. His biography appears after "Breaking the Cycle," which is found earlier in this chapter.

Prepared for Battle

"Are you sure you haven't
babysat for us before?"

Quite a Son-in-Law

A Jewish girl brings her fiancé home to meet her parents. After dinner, her mother tells her father to find out about the young man. He invites the fiancé into his study for schnapps.

"So, what are your plans?" the father asks the fiancé.

"I am a Torah scholar," he replies.

"A Torah scholar," the father says. "Admirable; but what will you do to provide a nice house for my daughter to live in, as she's accustomed to?"

"I will study," the young man replies, "and God will provide for us."

"And how will you buy her a beautiful engagement ring, such as she deserves?" asks the father.

"I will concentrate on my studies," the young man replies, "God will provide for us."

"And children?" asks the father. "How will you support children?"

"Don't worry, sir; God will provide," replies the fiancé.

The conversation proceeds like this, and each time the father questions, the fiancé insists that God will provide.

Later, the mother asks, "How did it go?" The father answers, "He has no job and no plans, but the good news is he thinks I'm God."

Which Father Knows Best?

In 1985, I entered the masters in theology program at Franciscan University of Steubenville in Ohio. Our second daughter, Martha, was born just two weeks before we packed up our belongings and moved to Steubenville. At that time, there were only two married students in the masters program and it was rare to find young children and infants on the campus. With a three-year-old and newborn, our family attracted quite a bit of attention among the students.

We regularly attended daily Mass as a family and often had plenty of volunteers to help with our children. Our two girls became quite popular with the students and priests who wanted to assure us that our children were a welcome addition to campus life.

While at Mass one evening, Martha began to fuss a bit during the reading of the Gospel. As Father began his homily, her fussing increased, but was at a level most would be able to tolerate. As I got up to take her out, Father interrupted his sermon and said, "Jim, you don't have to leave, she's not bothering us." I made a simple motion to Father to acknowledge his comment but continued toward the aisle.

Father repeated, this time with great compassion, "No, Jim, she really isn't a bother. You don't have to leave."

By this time, every eye in the church was on me, staring and awaiting my response. I understood that Father was trying to extend me every consideration and reassure me that my children were welcome at Mass. I didn't want to contradict Father, but knew I had to do the right thing as Martha's father.

"Actually, Father, I do need to go," I explained before the entire congregation. "She has a dirty diaper."

—Jim FritzHuspen

Jim FritzHuspen is the father of four children, aged fourteen to twenty-three. He is the administrator of Spirit of Life Parish in Mandan, North Dakota, where he has worked for the past eighteen years since graduating from Franciscan University of Steubenville with a master's degree in theology.

Chapter 5
A Father's Wisdom

Second Chance

When I realized the frigid water was robbing me of my oxygen, I thought to myself, "I'm going to die!" My little girl's face flashed before my mind and in a millisecond a dozen other thoughts filled my head. I'm a father; my daughter needs me! I should not have been so irresponsible. I should not have gone kayaking off-season and alone.

All winter long, I had enjoyed weekends at my vacation home in Pennsylvania's Pocono Mountains. Sometimes my daughter, Rachel, and my wife would join me; other times I'd go alone. Either way, my family understood and tolerated my restlessness, my constant craving for an adrenaline fix.

Snow is usually sparse in the Poconos by late March, indicating an end to another ski season. I was particularly fidgety one early spring weekend and decided I would place my kayak in the Lehigh River. My family implored me to hold off, but I ignored what I perceived to be their lack of faith in my athletic prowess.

Having enjoyed a successful career as a national martial arts champ, I was still at the top of my game. However, since I mastered my sport at a young age, I constantly sought after fresh challenges. Skiing and kayaking were just two in a series of new adventures for me.

So, against all advice, I took to the frigid river late in March. I had always kayaked the Lehigh in late spring or

early fall, but I was not prepared for what I was about to
face. The water flow was an unbelievable 3,200 cubic feet per
second, five times greater than what I had ever experienced. I
was only wearing a partial wet suit, and my boat was neither
large enough nor suitable for waters of this magnitude. But
the last of my boating sins would nearly cost me my life:
I went alone! Still, the eight-mile adventure was going as
planned. "Why was everyone so concerned?" I wondered.

About three miles down river, I approached an island of
trees and I wasn't sure if I should go to the right or the left.
My father always said, "Indecisiveness can kill you." At first
I decided to go right but at the last moment veered in the
opposite direction. It was too late. I swerved into the island
so hard that the boat skirt tore and water instantly filled
the kayak. I quickly jumped out. Hugging a tree with one
hand and my paddle in the other, I watched as my kayak
disappeared down the Lehigh. In frustration, I threw the
paddle in as well.

Yes, I was literally up a river without a paddle—or a
boat—but I had plenty of humble pie. There was no one
around for miles, and the distance from the island to either
shore was the same. Would I be as indecisive leaving the
island as I had been in my arrival?

Then I did the unthinkable. I deliberately let go of the
tree and jumped into the rushing river. About thirty yards
from shore I came up for air, but there wasn't any. This
defied logic, since my life jacket kept my head out of the
water. That's when I realized that the shock of thirty-two
degree water knocked the wind out of me. "Lord," I pleaded,
"Give me the strength to get through this for Rachel's sake."
I had no prior knowledge as to how I should react in such
a predicament, but what I did next saved my life. I plunged

my face back into the water and swam with every last bit of energy left in me. God was surely in control.

Only a miracle can explain the series of events that followed. I emerged from the icy water to find a tree limb hanging directly over me. I caught it and hung on for dear life while the raging river tugged at my body. Again petitioning God's help, I managed to pull myself onto the riverbank.

Freezing and in shock, I worked my way through the brush to the top of the snow-covered Lehigh gorge trail. Adrenaline kicked in and without thinking I began to run, soaking wet, through four inches of snow for more than five miles. Finally, I reached my friend who was waiting for me on the bank. He had expected me to arrive in the river, not on the path, but his stoic expression told me that he had a good idea about what might have happened. Instead of saying, "I told you so," he silently handed me a much-needed towel. "Whew," I shook my head and motioned toward the car. My friend considerately remained silent, allowing me to collect my emotions as we got into the car. He knew I would explain when I was ready, so he simply turned the heat up to the max and pulled away.

To keep a tear from running down my cheek I threw my head back against the headrest. The hot air blowing against my neck was a welcoming sensation. After a few seconds, I slowly closed my eyes and bowed my head as I called upon God once more. This time, I prayed that the Lord would forgive my haughtiness. Longing to see my wife and daughter again, I began to imagine the pain I might have caused if they were to have received a tragic phone call from a park ranger or state trooper. Holding back the tears, I prayed even harder. "Thank you, Lord," I began, "You have always been there when I needed you most. The branch that saved my life, that was your extended arm, wasn't it? Of course, it was! I needn't question you." The vividness with which I now imagined God's arm gave me chills. God had shed His grace on me countless times throughout my life, but this pivotal moment was the greatest of all eye openers.

—Daniel Pope

Daniel Pope is a master karate instructor, winning more than a hundred martial arts grand championships. He runs the Daniel Pope Karate Institutes in Lansdowne and Springfield, Pennsylvania, where he resides with his wife and daughter. Pope is also the co-author of The Adventures of Dayne Traveler, *an entertaining book of short stories based on his various endeavors.*

Lighten Up! It's Christmas!

As each did his job cleaning up after supper on Christmas Eve, our younger boys sang popular Christmas carols, often inserting their own silly lyrics in an attempt to gain the respect of their older siblings. With the last plate put away, floor swept, and garbage removed, my wife, Beverly, our six boys, and I gathered around the dining room table. I cracked open the Bible and began to read the account of Jesus' birth from the gospel of Matthew. It was important to me that my boys hear the true meaning of Christmas, for even back in 1973, the Holy Day had become too commercialized.

I had never been a big fan of the Santa Claus story, and this particular year, Bev and I had agreed to keep gifts to a bare minimum. We didn't want our boys to be marred by the secular adaptation of Christmas. Besides, times were tough. Two years earlier, I had been among the 10,000 Boeing Helicopter employees who bore the wrath of downsizing. Despite earning a master's in engineering from Yale, I was relying on food stamps as I struggled in the proprietorship of a new heating and cooling business about which I knew very little.

This trying time in my life was a test of faith, and I was more determined and convicted than ever in mine. In fact, I may have been a bit over-restrictive regarding all the trappings of Christmas, as I would come to learn.

Midway through the Nativity reading, I was interrupted by a knock at the door and a jingling sound, like sleigh bells. Having been self-employed for two years at this point, nothing surprised me—not even an interruption at eight p.m. on the night before Christmas.

With a sense of indifference, I got up to answer the door. Beverly and all six boys were in tow. They must have suspected that this was no ordinary call because the children were excitedly curious. I swung open the door and to everyone's amazement there stood a man in a red Santa suit, complete with beard, belt, and boots. He carried a large burlap bag, like an oversized potato sack, stuffed with presents. With the assistance of two men dressed in green, like elves, he handed gifts to each of my boys.

I was as stunned as the rest of the family by our unexpected intruder. Like an inquisitive child, I began to interrogate him. "Where are you from?" I asked. "The North Pole," he cogently replied. However, as I continued to pepper him with questions he cleverly evaded each one before finally saying, "I'm sorry; we have so much to do tonight. Merry Christmas."

With that, our surprise visitor was gone. Although we've had suspicions over the years as to who he might have been, we are still not exactly sure and I don't even want to know. I was, and remain, touched by the generosity of someone who must have been aware of our financial constraints, yet likely unaware that I was becoming too fervent in my approach to the faith.

The next day, Christmas morning, I received another surprise gift. My oldest son, Tom—who was fifteen at the time—presented gifts to Bev and me as well as to each of his younger brothers. Tom was sensitive to both our financial situation as well as my feelings about Christmas, but didn't want his younger brothers to be disappointed. So he planned ahead. He saved all the money he earned on his paper rout to buy presents. Though simple, the gifts Tom bought were more extravagant than the few Bev and I had purchased.

I couldn't remember a more meaningful Christmas. Despite my efforts to teach my children the true meaning of the holiday, I was on the receiving end of an education. Just as He was there through all the difficult times, God reined me in when I needed to keep things in perspective. Although it was my duty to provide for my children, I had to be open to the gifts that Providence would offer.

—Joseph M. Oliver

Joseph M. Oliver is a husband, father, and grandfather. A Connecticut native and one of seven children, Joe is the founder and chairman of Oliver Heating & Cooling in Morton, Pennsylvania. In 1997, he was ordained a deacon and serves Our Lady of Perpetual Help Church in the Archdiocese of Philadelphia.

A Child's Love

For some dads, remembering to verbally express their love to their children is tough. Oh, sure, going to soccer games and helping them with their homework counts, but what kids need is to actually hear the words "I love you." I make the effort to *tell* them individually I love them at least once each day.

Occasionally, I forget the impact those words can have, especially on a child. Recently, I was getting ready to run errands around town. My son Garrett asked to come along, so we both hopped into the car and began our mission. I turned on the radio to catch a basketball game.

The game was a good one and I listened intently to every play. During intermission, I checked the rear view mirror to make sure Garrett was still safe and sound in his car seat. What I saw surprised me.

Instead of the cheerful, happy face that usually smiled back at me, there was a dejected little boy staring out the window. His hands were cupped over his ears, apparently trying to drown out my basketball game. His eyes brimmed with sadness.

"Garrett," I called back to him. "What's wrong? Are you OK?"

"I'm just sad," he replied. I was puzzled. He'd seemed fine when we left the house. I asked him why he was so sad.

"Because, Daddy," his small voice quivered. "I was trying to tell you I love you but you couldn't hear me."

A knife sank into my heart. I think it twisted once, too. I had gotten so caught up in stealing some "me" time that I had completely ignored my child. I apologized and reassured Garrett that I loved him, too, very, very much. A child places a vast amount of importance on the words "I love you." I'll never forget Garrett's reminder.

—Robert Blodgett

An experienced writer and award-winning speaker, Robert Blodgett serves as director of communications for Peregrine Systems, Inc. Learning from his own struggles to place his family first while still climbing the corporate ladder, Blodgett has chronicled his personal stories in Family First (Tales of a Working Father). *He lives in San Diego with his wife, Celeste, and their four sons.*

A Father Speaks from the Grave

It was the day my fiancée and I announced our engagement. My mom was overjoyed at the news, as was my stepfather. Such an event is a milestone for the mother of an only son who was twenty-two years old. As such, it occurred to her that I had "become a man." That realization sparked in her the memory that years ago she had been given a solemn duty to discharge.

I remember being in the kitchen alone one evening. My mother walked in and handed me a letter copied onto old mimeograph paper, the likes of which I had not seen since kindergarten. The seven pages were still folded, evidence of an envelope since discarded.

"What's this?" I asked.

"It's something I should have given you years ago," my mother said. "It's a letter from your father. He wrote it to you from Vietnam soon after he arrived there, just in case something were to happen to him. You were little at the time, of course. He said that if he didn't return from the war, I was to give it to you when you became a man. I forgot about it, to tell you the truth, although I thought I never would. When you and Claudia announced your engagement, it jogged my memory. It has been years since I read or even thought about it. In reading it again, I realize that I should have given it to you a long time ago. I'm sorry."

It is hard to describe how jolting were her words. You would think that I would have been ecstatic. Instead, I was in shock. It was too overwhelming. My mind sort of dazed. The letter in my hand seemed like a mysterious package with the potential to explode, depending on what it said.

While these things were going through my mind, my body was having a reaction of its own. My face paled. I went a bit numb. My hands turned cold and began to tremble slightly. I took the letter and went to my room. I was completely unable to say anything to my mother beyond a quiet, "Thank you."

There's something confusing about receiving a letter from your deceased father who had been gone so long that you don't have a solitary memory of him. What I knew about him I had learned by asking questions of my mother, my grandmother, and my aunts. I had read newspaper clippings and looked through scrapbooks. I had made peace with the fact that these tidbits were as much as I would ever know about my dad. There was no reason to expect more; certainly no reason to expect a personal letter seventeen years after a landmine ended his life.

I sat stunned in my room. Finally, after a few minutes, I managed to unfold the pages. They were hand-written. I felt privileged to see his handwriting. I had not seen it before. Some words were hard to decipher, but worth the effort in the personality they afforded over type-written pages.

I got through only a couple of lines before I had to stop and fold it back up. I wasn't ready. My head had not the slightest idea how to take in the letter. Part of me was afraid to read it. I was afraid that with one quarter of my life behind me, it would not please him—that the path I had chosen would not have his blessing. By that stage in my life, I had adjusted to not having to take into account my father's approval or disapproval. Now, all of a sudden, I might have to.

At the same time, I felt humbled that I was even getting the chance to know my father's thoughts. I wondered, "How many other boys would have the opportunity to read a letter from a father they never knew?"

I set the pages on my desk and went back downstairs. My mom noticed my melancholy mood and asked, "Did you read the letter?"

"Not yet," I replied, without offering an explanation. I didn't have one. I hardly understood it, myself.

That brief exchange was enough to drive me back upstairs where I sat down and read the letter straight through. The words took on an almost sacred quality. This is part of what I read:

Dear Doug:

Your old man is writing this letter tonight because he feels the urge to share some basic thoughts with his only son. You are a very little boy at this writing, but the years will pass rapidly and someday soon you will be a young man facing the realities of life.

I fully expect to be around in the years to come and hope to assist you on your path through life; however, one never knows what the future will bring.

Someday, you will have to decide on a career. Many well-meaning people will offer their sincere advice and you will undoubtedly be quite confused. The choice of your life's work is equally as important as choosing a life's mate. Before you can do either, you must decide what you are yourself, as a person. As the years go by, you will soon discover whether you are outward or timid, adventuresome or docile, ambitious or complacent. It is no sin to be one or the other; but it is extremely important that you discover what you are—not what at some moment in life you may think you would like to be.

After you decide what you are, think about what you would like to be within the personality and innate intelligence you possess; and then, unless you lack all ambition, pick a goal several steps higher than what you think you can achieve and work like the very devil to achieve it. Remember, son, the tallest and straightest trees grow in crowded forests where they must each individually reach for the very sun that enables them to grow into large and proud trees, in competition with the other trees. Scrub oaks only grow by themselves where they have no competition to spur them on.

Many people . . . exist in a dream world . . . I have heard ministers and teachers condemn the war in Vietnam on many grounds they sincerely believe to be unquestionably valid. Their words of complaint have scant meaning when I watch people going to the Catholic church nearby on Sunday and realize that until a few weeks ago, this was impossible because of Communist terrorism and military operations. I watch students, little boys like yourself, walk to school each morning under the protection of armed troops. I know that no schools or churches are allowed to operate in parts of this district I advise because they are under Communist control . . .

It was said centuries ago that for every man willing to lead, 1,000 wait to be led. Your father is very proud of this army Green he wears and would not trade his life as an Infantry Officer for any other endeavor, whatsoever. I hope someday you can say the same thing about what you have done for the first dozen years after achieving manhood.

Doug, you are a very intelligent boy and you have an extremely kind disposition. Should something happen to me, and I hope to still be serving in the world's action spots when you are my present age, do not try to emulate a way of life that may not be suitable to your own particular make-up. I do hope you will choose a way of life that holds some potential for helping to make this a better world. . .

*Regardless of what career you choose, I do challenge you
to do your part in defending the rights you have inherited. Do
not rationalize and try to say you are doing your part if your
conscience tells you otherwise. One must develop self-respect
before he can hope to attain it from others.*

*Ten years from now, let's you and I sit down and discuss this
far too wordy letter . . . and learn from each other, as I am sure
that by then there will be much your old dad can learn from
you.*

Love,
Dad

When I finished reading the letter, it was if the weight
of the world had been lifted from my shoulders. I was not
faced with trying to rebuild my life, after all. Instead, my
dad had affirmed me, citing traits he had seen in me even
when I was a little boy. His words were encouraging and
motivating, not scolding or dogmatic. Instead of trying to
persuade me to follow in his footsteps (which I had begun to
do—even applying to West Point, only to withdraw) he held
up virtues for which I could strive no matter what career I
chose. It felt good that, after all those years, I had some basis
for thinking my dad would have been proud of me.

I had received my father's blessing. It had come after
many years, even from beyond the grave, but it had finally
come.

It is my wish that every father would realize the innate
and powerful impact he has upon his kids' lives. He has the
potential he can endow toward self-esteem or self-hatred;
toward confidence or insecurity. It is my wish that fathers
would never miss a chance to plant seeds of encouragement
in young hearts. As my father said: "I fully expect to be
around in the years to come and hope to assist you in your

path through life; however, one never knows what the future will bring."

—J. Douglas Burford

Dr. J. Douglas Burford trusts that his father would agree that he has "chosen a way of life that helps to make this world a better place." He is pastor of the Ward Parkway Presbyterian Church in Kansas City, Missouri, is married to a perfect angel, and has three children of whom he could not be more proud. In addition to leading people in Christian community, he enjoys speaking and writing.

Lessons from on High

It was 8:40 a.m. on a Sunday morning, and I was on top of the roof of our new house wondering exactly how I was going to get down. Let me explain. As my wife, Amy, and I were leaving for church, Amy realized we'd forgotten something. While I don't remember what we forgot, I do remember what happened. Amy went to open the door and realized she'd locked it—and we didn't have a key.

Suddenly two adults had an opportunity to problem-solve a situation and figure out the best way to get inside the house. Amy's first thought was to go around the perimeter of our home to see if any windows looked open. My first idea was, *Ooooh, I could climb the scaffolding left by the builders in the back and get up on the roof!*

How my idea was going to help us get into the house, I had no clue; it simply sounded fun!

It took me about 2.5 minutes to climb the outside of the scaffolding to make it onto the roof. Once atop, I realized how beautiful our property was, how nice the lake looked, and that our children looked like tiny ants from such a high vantage point. This only distracted me from my initial reason for climbing on the roof, which was to get inside the house—not on top of it!

I scooted down one of the pitches of the roof and found myself slightly stuck in a place that didn't feel too safe. Now I was focused—but not on how to get into the house. This time it was on how to get off the roof.

How did I get into this mess? I wondered. Then I heard Amy's voice from thirty feet below.

"Michael? Where are you? I got it, let's go."

While I was being manly and climbing the roof, Amy managed to get into the house, get what she wanted, and was now ready to leave for church.

But there was still one problem. I was stuck on the roof!

"Michael!" she shouted again.

"I'm right here!" I shouted back. I watched her look around—at ground level—to see where my voice was coming from. Of course, with any normal individual, that would have been a good place to look. But she must have forgotten my "uniqueness" as a man.

"Where are you?" she asked.

"Right here!" I replied trying to draw her attention upward.

As she finally tracked my voice upward onto the roof, her eyes said it all: what in the world is my husband doing up there?!

I'll never forget that look.

I tried to explain why I was up there, but she just wanted me off the roof and in the car so we could go to church, like a normal family. I told her it wasn't going to be that easy. So while she and the kids waited for me to figure out how to make it down, I managed a brilliant plan and was off the roof in time to make it to church.

Most married women have probably experienced something like this before. OK, maybe their husbands didn't climb the roof, but I'm sure they did something else that made their wives climb the walls. And I'm sure it made perfect sense to the husbands—at the time.

But I made an important discovery that day. I learned that in my "manly" desire to be the knight in shining armor, I sometimes make hasty—and dumb—decisions.

On that Sunday morning, all ended well with no one getting hurt. But I realize that if I rush any decision—whether it's getting into a locked house or something on a grander scale—I need to keep a cool head, discuss things with my wife, and often, seek counsel. I need to consider: what does God want me to do?

It probably doesn't involve climbing onto a roof.

—Michael Smalley

Michael Smalley and his wife, Amy, both hold masters degrees in clinical psychology from Wheaton College in Chicago. For the past ten years, they have spoken live to millions of people around the world. They have authored or coauthored the relationship advice books Communicating with Your Teen, The Men's Relational Toolbox, *and* Don't Date Naked. *They have been married for eleven years and have three children, Cole, Reagan, and David. For more information, visit the Smalley Family Outreach website at www.smalleyoutreach.org.*

Whacked on the Head with Love

Despite the fact that I work for the Church, I can be a bit of a skeptic when it comes to "things supernatural." I surely believe that God exists and all that the Church teaches, but I sometimes struggle when it comes to things providential. In short, I try not to see a miracle or sign around every corner. There have been times, however, when God has hit me over the head with a 2" x 4" beam of grace—revealing His sign so clearly that it would be spiritually negligent not to believe.

Such an event happened to me not too long ago. I was sitting in my car on a cold December morning outside my office. I was on my cell phone with a friend who is a great devotee of St. Maximilian Kolbe. I needed advice about some strife I was experiencing as a father and husband. My friend then said, "You still live across the street from St. Max church, right?" I responded affirmatively. He then suggested to me that I turn to St. Maximilian in intercessory prayer. "He gave his life for a father. He knows your struggles. Ask for his prayers."

At that very moment, I looked out the window and saw a light blue tractor trailer with the words "Kolbe Kolbe" printed in massive blue letters on the side.

"You're not going to believe this," I said excitedly. "A truck just drove by with the word 'Kolbe' written twice on it. These two words must have been seven feet tall." My friend confidently said that it undoubtedly confirmed his advice to me to turn to Kolbe for intercessory prayer.

I had never heard of a secular company called Kolbe, nor ever seen this truck before with the massive words Kolbe Kolbe. What were the odds that I would see this truck at the exact moment I was being advised to ask St. Maximilian Kolbe to pray for my intentions?

Since I had never heard of this company before, I felt compelled to find out more about it. I walked into my office and jumped on the Internet. I typed in the words "Kolbe truck" into my Google search engine. A second later I saw "Kolbe and Kolbe Millwork" pop onto my screen. Not only did God hit me with a 2" x 4", but He delivered it in a wood truck.

—Matthew Pinto

Matthew Pinto is the co-creator and an editor of the Amazing Grace *series. His biography appears at the end of the book.*

Hot Shot Dad

Rolling Green Golf Course in Springfield, Pennsylvania, was one of my company's commercial clients. I own a heating and cooling business, but in the early days I was also the repairman.

So, when the club's general manager, Colonel Shawn, called me on a hot summer day and said the restaurant's big walk-in freezer stopped running, I responded right away. It was a condenser problem. Piece of cake!

My son Rob, who was seven at the time, was interested in learning the trade so I brought him along. We got the unit running almost immediately. I patted myself on the back, quite smug in my ability to wrap up the job so easily. I clearly had the magic touch, or so I thought.

With my index finger pressed against my forehead, I leaned into Rob and gloatingly commented, "Sometimes it's what's upstairs that earns you money, not hard work."

At that very moment, a large lightening bolt flashed across the daytime sky, accompanied almost simultaneously with an intense crack of thunder. The Scripture verse "Pride goes before a fall" instantly came to mind.

The jolt interrupted power to the golf course, wreaking havoc on the unit we had just fixed. It stopped dead! The job then became laborious and dirty.

More important than learning how to fix a condenser, both my son and I learned an enormous lesson in humility: Don't act big – the proud are humbled.

The real magic touch comes from above.

—Joseph M. Oliver

Joseph M. Oliver's biography appears after "Lighten Up, It's Christmas!" which is found earlier in this chapter.

Broken Toys

"I bought a bunch of broken toys today.
These should save the kids a lot of time and effort."

Cost Versus Value

I remember laughing when we were expecting our first child and I heard how much money we needed to save to ensure a proper "nest egg" for our future children and our retirement. I was a radio news reporter at a CBS station in Portland, Oregon. My wife, Patti, was just graduating with honors from a masters of public administration program at Portland State University. We had met in the Peace Corps, drove a British two-seater convertible, and spent our weekends as a young, carefree, childless couple. We enjoyed cross-country skiing in the Cascade Mountains during the winter and backpacked on mountain trails or looked for agates on Oregon's white sand beaches in the summer.

But shortly after we had our first child, most people thought we had lost our marbles. I quit my well-paying job and Patti took her hard-earned masters degree to become Jesuit volunteers on the Flathead Indian Reservation in Ronan, Montana. We traded in the sports car for a Ford Escort, traded life in a high-rise apartment building in downtown Portland for a tiny crumbling home. It was not the advice the financial adviser had in mind for us.

Trading in the "good life" for something more spiritually meaningful affected how I experienced fatherhood. Money took a back seat. Like any loving father would say, it was the most exciting, life-changing moment in his life. With most "high point" experiences, people want more. A great meal, a fantastic vacation, or a favorite movie are all enjoyable things that create the desire for more. But when it comes to children, it's not unusual for people to say "no more" In many cases, it boils down to money: "We can't afford another."

I came across a piece on the Internet that the government recently calculated the cost of raising a child from birth to eighteen at $160,140 for the average family. With a price tag like that, no wonder some families reel from sticker shock. Bargain shopping and economizing make children much less expensive, but even at full price, they are still a bargain.

While some financial advisors might consider having another child to be fiscally foolish, it actually depends on what sort of wealth we are talking about. You can put $160,140 into something tangible like land, stocks, or some other investment, but it can drop in value and you can't take it with you. If you put your money in a child, that investment is everlasting.

In addition you get:

- Naming rights.
- To be seen as "god-like" in the eyes of your children.
- Someone to give bear hugs.
- Companionship and free entertainment.
- More hugs and kisses than an accountant can tally.
- Someone to open up your world to the wonder of trees, bugs, rainbows, thunder storms, and garbage trucks.
- A true-blue fan
- Someone to laugh at your jokes.
- A reason to still play at the playground.
- Someone who appreciates the faces you carve on pumpkins.
- A reason to celebrate Father's Day.
- To be a hero just for being taller and stronger than Mom.
- To witness home runs that were hit over the fence with a plastic bat from the comfort of your backyard.

- The opportunity to be the best baseball or soccer coach in the world.
- A front row seat for driver's training.
- A free education in the assembly of bikes and large plastic toys from China.
- To speak for God as you love and discipline your child.
- More real power than superheroes to fix things, take the family on a vacation, police a teen, ground them for eternity, and then return their freedom again.
- To hear a child squeal "I love you, Daddy!"

And then, to top off all of the earthly delights, you get the joys of grandchildren.

—Mark Armstrong

Mark Armstrong is a co-editor of Amazing Grace for Fathers. *His biography appears at the end of the book.*

Dadisms

Like most men who have a wrench-tight grasp on the English language, my father is neither loud nor outspoken. He has no need to be when a word or phrase can say it all.

As a father, he could (and still can) deliver one-liners that would make my three brothers and me shake with laughter or shake in our boots—depending on the situation. As kids, it was like having Bill Cosby as a dad when times called for rousing joy ("Dad is great, he gives us chocolate cake!") or Clint Eastwood when we deserved to be put in our place ("Go ahead, make my day.").

Over the years, my father developed a repertoire of these signature phrases. Classic dadisms, I call them. Take five minutes and I bet you can think of a dozen sayings your own father popularized.

Recently, one of my older brothers and I had a good laugh over the fact that we now involuntarily blurt out some of those same lines to our own kids. It shows the real influence that fathers have on their children and—more to the point—it proves that we were actually listening back then.

To have a little fun with this, I asked my brothers to help me catalog our dad's dadisms. Well, that was like asking three wolves to help me count the sheep. They were more than happy to oblige. What burst forth was a litany of teachings, encouragements, confidence-builders, admonishments, and veiled threats. The whole gamut of fatherly wisdom; a philosophy of life.

First, he was the purveyor of practical advice:

"Get in or get out." This applied to an open back door and an open refrigerator. "Just because you don't pay the gas and electric bills, that doesn't mean you should waste energy," he'd tell us as we alternately let the cold air into the house and out of the fridge, deciding if we wanted to play football or have some milk. As I realized later, this sage advice applies to life in general. Make your choice, then move ahead.

"Quit talking about it and do it." It doesn't have quite the same ring as Nike's famed "Just Do It" campaign, but it's the same concept. My father likes accomplishment and action. Be smart and make an educated decision, yes—but once you've made the decision, act on it.

"How 'bout putting some light on the subject." For some reason, my brothers and I had a habit of doing our homework in the dark. Leave it to my dad to constantly warn us about the risk of going blind. We heard this phrase—which was clearly more of a command than a question—at least twice a day for our entire childhoods. It's actually quite good advice: put yourself in an environment that leads to success.

"Oh, those bases on balls." My father passed down his love of baseball to my brothers and me. It's something that binds us to this day. Something else that happens to this day: watch a game with my dad and you'll hear him utter this phrase every time a pitcher walks a batter. He hates a free pass. You earn everything in life.

He was also the voice of discipline:

"You better stop crying ... or I'll give you something to cry about." My dad sure had the market covered on phrases that discouraged tears. I think this one was the most effective. I don't ever remember finding out what that "something" was that he was going to "give" us, so I guess the line worked.

"Quit" and "Knockitoff!" As you can imagine, raising four active boys may have been trying at times. Between our bouts of wrestling on the floor and games of verbal one-upsmanship, my brothers and I rarely gave my father a moment's rest when he got home from work. An unambiguous "Quit" or "Knockitoff!" usually bought him enough time to glance at the sports page.

"Don't make me turn this car around." With four boys crammed in the back seat of the car, at least one child was always crossing into the imaginary line we had drawn between us. This resulted in retaliatory action by the offended party. Whether we were a block from home or 700 miles away on vacation, you always took my dad's threat seriously. He would, in fact, turn this car around.

Finally, he was—and is—the guy who's always there to encourage you, no matter what:

"Keep on plugging." To this day, most telephone conversations with my father end with this phrase. It's probably my favorite expression. Not only does it encourage you to keep working hard in your professional and personal life, but it also implies that he approves and is proud of what you're doing. Nothing means more than that to a son.

"It never hurts to ask." My dad made his living as a college fundraiser. His working motto was "It never hurts to ask," a saying he adopted from my younger brother who, as a child, once presented a detailed, 12-page wish list to be mailed to Santa. The lesson here is that nothing is impossible. If you have an idea, go for it. Not asking or not trying is the only thing you'll regret.

"Another day, another dollar." We heard this phrase every single day my father returned from work. It may sound like the crass talk of capitalism, but my father is not about the cash. He is about the hard work. He is about the dedication. He is about making every day count and giving your all every time out.

"Payback time, buddy!" As a grandfather, this has emerged as his latest classic. If you tell him about sleepless nights with the baby or a kid who acted up in church, he's sure to ooze with delight, "Payback time, buddy!" Like I say, he's there for you no matter what.

In honor of Dad, I hope you'll salute your old man by rattling off some of his favorite sayings. Let him know you were listening. More importantly, take the wisdom of your father and live by it. Pass it on to the next generation. You'll soon see how your own children will benefit.

—Brian Kantz

Brian Kantz, author of "The Newbie Dad" column in Western New York Family magazine, is a stay-at-home dad and writer. He lives in Amherst, New York, with his wife, Amy, and son, Brendan. Visit him online at www. briankantz.com.

Fatherly Advice to Newlyweds

My advice to the Newlywed?
While you're young, use your head!
Have a baby...
Have a few!
I don't mean just one,
or even two.
What about four?
How about eight?
(Making babies is really great!)

Don't worry about braces,
or college, or clothes.
Their every need
God already knows.
Then when you're old,
in time of need,
with no more clamoring mouths to feed,
look to your children
that you (and God) made,
to be your joy,
comfort, and aid.

Your babies today
are your greatest treasure.
You will receive
in the amount you measure.

God's greatest gift
to husband and wife?
A newborn baby.
An eternal life!

—Dr. Brian J. Kopp

Dr. Brian Kopp is a podiatrist practicing in Johnstown, PA. He and his wife, Sue, home school their three children. This poem is his sole attempt at poetry, originally written on the back of a napkin at the wedding reception of a college roommate. The Kopp family prays daily for the blessing of more children."

Knot Passing up the Opportunity

"Dad, I need your help," my son said as he entered the room.

Hearing that admission from my almost seventeen-year-old warmed my heart. It made me feel important. At this stage in his teenage-hood, that stage of rapidly growing independence, it was nice to hear that my son needed me for something.

"Do you need money?"

"No. At least not now," he said.

"Help with your homework?"

He snickered. I think the last time that I was able to help him with his homework we were looking for rhyming words in magazines.

"I need to learn how to tie a necktie," he said.

He had several important events coming up where he needed to dress up. I mean dress up by adult standards, not teenage standards. A teenager's idea of getting dressed up usually means wearing clothes that are not retrieved from the hamper and not wearing Nikes.

I was happy to help during this turning point in my son's life. There are several things that boys should only learn from their fathers: shaving, throwing a curveball, jump starting a dead car battery, and tying a necktie.

I grabbed a couple of ties from my closet and stood next to my son in front of a mirror. We went through the drill over and over again. When another one of my sons entered the room he grabbed a necktie and began tying. Then my daughter joined us. Necktie Tying 101 was in full swing.

"How's this look?" one son asked.

"Like you've been in a fight. Try it again."

"What about this?" the other one asked.

"Is that a Windsor knot or an origami swan? Keep trying."

"Mine looks the best, doesn't it Daddy?" my daughter asked.

"Sweetheart, it's a necktie, not a bow tie. Keep trying."

Although most guys do not exactly like wearing a necktie, it actually serves several functions: it covers missing shirt buttons, it gives guys something to violently tug on when angry at their bosses, and tying a necktie gives men something to do when they want to waste time before attending formal events.

Neckties do serve one more purpose: they give fathers the chance to spend time with their sons to hand down something once handed down to him by his father. They give us memories and bonding and a chance to give fatherly wisdom. Not bad for a simple necktie.

—Tim Herrera

Tim Herrera is the author of several stories in this book. His biography appears after "Breaking the Cycle" in Chapter 4 - A Father's Humor.

To Stephen, On His Graduation

Dear Son,

It seems like last Wednesday that you graduated from kindergarten with a Life Saver dangling from your cardboard hat. I congratulated you then on waiting until the final prayer to crunch the candy. And I also congratulate you today on an even greater achievement: graduation from high school.

Your mother and I felt like singing the "Hallelujah Chorus" when you seized that diploma, for there were times we wondered if you'd stop playing hockey, or baseball, or "Age of Empires" long enough to finish crucial assignments. Like me, you suffer from Attention Deficit Disorder, a wonderful condition full of constant surprises, but something teachers are still learning to appreciate. Despite these distractions, you have passed enough tests, written enough essays, and dissected enough frogs. I'm proud of you. When I was your age, I was madly in love with your mother. I'm glad to see that you are not experiencing those glorious distractions yet.

Some of your peers accepted honors today and it's important that you learn to rejoice with them. We Callaways were seldom singled out for academic awards, partly because we wanted to give the other students a chance, and partly because, as your grandfather once said, when they were handing out brains, we were at the buffet table loading up on ham. I made the Horror Role twice, but never the Honor Roll. And so, in the absence of other honors, I wish to bestow upon you three distinguished awards, with some sponsors you may recognize.

1. **The Pulitzing My Leg Prize.** Solomon once wrote that laughter is better than Prozac, and you have proved him right. You have invented hilarious faces, said things we still can't believe, and brought abundant humor into our home. You have put gum in my hair, soap in my toothbrush, and Kool-Aid in the showerhead. People ask where I get ideas for my books. They need look no further than you and your siblings. Never forget that one laugh is better than three tablespoons of bran flakes. Laughter is a holy gift from a loving God. Those who laugh the hardest don't laugh because life is easy, but because they have felt God's hand of mercy on their shoulders.

2. **The Callaway Golf Award.** People wonder how I can endure a game that rewards perseverance, courage, and devotion—with ulcers. The reason is simple. I love to be with my kids. We have peeled divots from dozens of golf courses together. And we have learned disconcerting things about our sinful nature. In fact, sometimes we've been so mad at ourselves that we've forgotten to hate our enemies. I love the way you put everything into each swing. And I don't begrudge the fact you are now hitting the ball farther than I. This world won't be a better place until kids are an improvement on their parents, so go ahead and hit it hard. Your generation is characterized by apathy. May that never be said of you. Keep lunging at life and whacking it dead center.

3. **The GAP Award (God Answers Prayer).** Eighteen years ago your birth changed my life. I was humbled with a sense of my shortcomings. Unprepared for the intensity of my desire to see you walk with God. I began praying a simple prayer back then: that you would fall in love with Jesus and never get over it. I have seen Him answer in

marvelous ways. Lately my prayer is even more basic: That
you would see the awfulness of sin and the greatness of God.
In traveling to a few hundred speaking engagements with
me, hauling my luggage through countless airports, there are
few things you haven't seen Satan doing. But you've also seen
God at work. Remember the men's retreat where a convicted
murderer covered in tattoos hugged you hard? I suspect you
do. "Follow God," he said, "and you won't end up like me. I
never knew my father. Thank God for yours."

I've accepted a few honors in my day, but none comes close
to the honor of being your dad. Twenty-five years ago today
your mother and I walked the same aisle, graduating from the
same school. We have found every promise of God to be true;
every day He has been faithful. He will do the same for you.

I suspect you saw my tears today as you and two friends
sang the closing song at the graduation ceremony. I couldn't
help myself. I cried because I love you. I cried because the
words sum it up so well: "Your grace still amazes me, your
love is still a mystery. Every day I get on my knees, your
grace still amazes me."

Keep singing it. Keep living it. All the way Home.

With love, admiration, and applause,
Dad

PS: We hope you enjoy the cash, the books, and the Life
Savers. One of these days I'll return the gum, the soap, and
the Kool-Aid—when you least expect it.

—Phil Callaway

*Phil Callaway's biography appears after his story "Blindsided" in Chapter
2 – A Father's Strength.*

Chapter 6
A Father's Character

Highway Hero

Driving home through the beach town of Costa Mesa, California, one Sunday evening in July, I was lost in my thoughts. As an aspiring filmmaker and actor, my mind wandered to some projects I was working on.

In 2003, I had not yet met with success. I suspected that my parents were worried about their 29-year-old son. My father was successful in real estate and I knew he hoped for the best for me. He and Mother left Egypt in 1969 to escape religious persecution. As Coptic Orthodox Christians, my parents always instilled in me that our religious values must always be reflected in the life we lived. "Have the courage to do what's right," my dad taught me.

I was suddenly snapped out of my reverie when I realized the car on the street just ahead of me was completely stopped. I quickly shifted lanes, assuming it was just a crazy driver.

I slowed down to pass the car and then braked. Something was terribly wrong. The car's front end was completely smashed in. The car looked like it had been rolled. Shattered glass and pieces of metal littered the street.

I looked up and down the street, expecting there to be a police car or emergency vehicle on its way. Cars sped by without even slowing up. I could not just pass by. Someone could be hurt in there. I pulled over to the side of the road and cautiously approached the car, fearful of what I might find inside.

There was a man in the car about my age, slumped against the steering wheel. My heart beat wildly. *Was he still alive?* I wondered. I pulled at the crumpled door, but it would not budge. Gingerly, I put my arm through the window, avoiding the shards of glass, and shook him. The unconcious man gave a slight moan.

A tow truck stopped on the other side of the road. "Is he OK?" the driver asked.

"He's not moving," I shouted over the steady stream of cars that whizzed by. "Can you radio for help?" Traffic kept rolling by. When a curious driver rolled down his window, I pleaded for help: "Call 911!"

Suddenly, something exploded under the car's accordian-like hood. Black smoke billowed out. The tow-truck driver rushed over and sprayed the hood with a fire extinguisher but it had no effect. The flames grew unabated. A voice from his truck radio called for him. "Keep on spraying!" he yelled to me, and ran back to his truck.

Fully extending my arm with the extinguisher straight in front of me, I moved closer to the flames. The putrid fumes of oil and wiring burned my nostrils and stung my face. Still the flames grew. They were moving into the car, headed toward the front seat. I shook with fear. The car was certain to blow at any minute.

"Come quickly!" I pleaded to the tow-truck driver. We frantically tried to yank the driver's door open to no avail. It would not even budge. I felt utterly helpless.

The thick black cloud of smoke stung our eyes and forced us back. I looked around frantically. What was taking the fire trucks so long? I knew there was little time left. At any moment the car would explode into an inferno, instantly killing the man inside.

A low moan came from the man. I could not just stand there and watch him die. "We've got to help him," I shouted. The truck driver and I again gave our all against the car door. Our arms shook as we tried to push our muscles beyond their abilities. The door was unmovable. We were again driven back by the flames that had reached the back seat, getting dangerously close to the gas tank.

Panting and shaking, I wiped the sweat from my forhead. We were helpless. What could we possibly do? But then I heard my dad's voice in my head: "Have the courage to do what's right." I always knew that meant turning to God. No mere human could save this man now. "Lord, only You can save him," I prayed. "Lend me Your strength."

Instictively, I filled my lungs with fresh air and then charged through the black smoke. The truck driver was right behind me. I pulled on the window frame with renewed strength while he yanked the bottom of the door. Suddenly, we lurched backward when the door flew open.

I lunged back to the car and grabbed the man's arm. "Unbuckle your seat belt!" I screamed. "I can't reach it!" Amazingly, he managed to release it. The truck driver and I dragged him out of the encroaching inferno. Holding him up, we stumbled across the street to safety. Just as we reached the other side, the whole front seat exploded into flames. Seconds later, the gas tank blew up into a black and orange ball of fire. The force actually knocked me back.

It was then that the fire truck, ambulance, and police sirens pierced the night air. Paramedics rushed over to the injured man and placed him on a stretcher. He seemed to be coming around.

"Is he going to be all right?" I asked.

Lifting him into the ambulance, one of the paramedics answered, "Looks like second and third degree burns. But he ought to be OK, thanks to you guys." Then the ambulance sped away.

The truck driver and I stood there shell-shocked as the firemen hosed down the car. I looked at him and gave him a bear hug. This stanger and I had just saved a life. I was still numb when I got back into my car and continued on my way home. As the shock and adreniline wore off, I began to process the surreal event I had just played a part in.

One moment I was driving along thinking about my life, and the next moment I was saving the life of another. Alone, I had failed again and again. All seemed lost. But then the words of my own father commanded me to do what was right—to turn to my Heavenly Father when all seemed lost. It was not just the work of the truck driver and me that saved the man—it was the work of my two fathers.

—John Abiskaron

John Abiskaron lives with his wife, Gehan, in Hollywood, California. He acts in movie and theater and also works in film and video production, covering sporting events, and in radio production.

A Father for My Son

"Have a good day," I said nervously to my son, Dustin, as I dropped him off at his kindergarten classroom. I watched lovingly as he bounced into the room. My five-year-old son was "all boy," full of energy and spunk.

But Dustin was not just a typical boy with boundless energy. He was becoming defiant and acting out. His teacher had complained to me that Dustin was often uncooperative in the classroom. The source of Dustin's difficulties were no mystery to me. As a single mother, I knew Dustin was an "at risk" boy. Without a father in his life, our family was out of balance. Even though my son was only five, he knew it innately.

One day, after another bad note from the teacher, I sat down with Dustin. "What's going on?" I asked.

"I hate school," Dustin responded as usual. But on this day, Dustin revealed why he was acting out. "The other boys just talk about the fun stuff they do with their dads," he sobbed. "Why do I have to be the only one without a dad?"

My heart sank. His father had left us before Dustin was born. As he grew, I tried to fill the void by playing sports and Nintendo, and providing plenty of boy-related activities. But it was not enough. I often watched Dustin wistfully gaze at other boys with their fathers. His hurt was coming out in anger and defiance both at home and in school.

"He needs a strong male influence," his teacher advised. I knew it, but what was I to do? There were no male relatives nearby. I tried to find opportunities for Dustin to be around other men, but without a real relationship between them, it made no difference.

How will I ever manage him as he gets older? I wondered
fearfully. Just asking him to clean his room or trying to get
him in bed on time usually turned into a big power struggle.
I also knew that it was not just Dustin who had the problem;
it was me, too. I felt sorry for him, so I had a hard time
being as firm as he needed me to be. My heart broke for
my poor son with no Daddy to tuck him in at night or
take him fishing. It wasn't his fault that he had no dad to
admire. In the end, my pity and his strong will were a bad
combination.

My attempts to bring faith into Dustin's life were also
rejected. One Sunday, after an exhausting struggle with
his unruly behavior during a church service, I gave up.
Unfortunately, I was not rooted firmly enough in my own
faith to put more effort into making it appealing to him. Not
only did Dustin not have an earthly father in his life, but due
to my own weak faith, he was missing his Heavenly Father
as well.

But God is always loving and generous. During a
moment of despair and fear for my son, I cried out to him.
"Lord, what can I do for Dustin? What can I give him to
make things better?" I prayed. "Dear God, please don't let
my son get lost."

Shortly after this prayer, my boss mentioned to me that
he volunteered with the Big Brother/Big Sister program
that matches kids in need of role models with adult mentors.
"Maybe Dustin could benefit from getting matched up with
a big brother," he suggested.

I had never considered this program. Dustin and I were
so vulnerable. How could I be sure that we would not go
from the frying pan into the fire should some unscrupulous
volunteer have bad motives? I mulled over the possibility and
expressed my misgivings. "Getting accepted as a volunteer

is like a top secret security clearance," my boss explained. I was working in the military at the time, so this comparison reassured me.

When I asked Dustin if he was interested, he perked up. "Would my Big Brother take me fishing?" he asked.

"You bet," I promised, hoping such would be the case.

My guard was up when Dustin's Big Brother, Bill Cafey, walked into my living room and sat on the couch. Dustin eyed him warily, too. Bill was married with two daughters; one in college and one in high school. *Why is he doing this?* I wondered. *Is this just going to be a resume filler for him? Will he put in his time and then leave Dustin abandoned again?*

"Do you like fishing?" Bill asked. My heart skipped a beat. It was the perfect question. Dustin shyly nodded.

"I never had a son," Bill explained. "I'm looking forward to having a little guy to have fun with."

Bill seemed nice enough and he had said all the right things, but the verdict was still out. Yet, I had no choice but to take a chance. "God, please take care of him," I prayed, hoping that Dustin would not one day get hurt or disappointed by Bill.

Dustin began spending Saturday afternoons with Bill. They went fishing or to the park or to a ball game. "Did you have fun?" I always asked when Dustin returned.

"Yeah, sure," he would shrug. I was a little disappointed with Dustin's lack of enthusiasm.

Isn't this what he wanted? I wondered. Three months into the relationship, Dustin still showed little enthusiasm, until one Saturday when Bill was late.

"Isn't he coming?" Dustin asked repeatedly. When he caught sight of Bill's car pulling up, he excitedly announced, "He's here!"

So he really does care, I realized. Dustin had likely been carefully guarding his emotions, but it was clear now that Bill mattered to him. It seemed that Dustin also mattered to Bill. Whenever he traveled on business, postcards arrived at our house.

"I'll be home soon," one postcard said. "We'll go fishing when I get back."

Receiving mail from Bill was a thrill for my young son. "He's my best friend," Dustin announced.

But Bill became much more than a mere friend. He became a surrogate father to Dustin. When Dustin was lagging behind in the first grade, Bill set some rules. "If your homework isn't done, we'll just stay and work on it," he determined. Dustin was not pleased with the stern Bill. He pouted. But once he realized Bill meant business, Dustin got down to work. After all, he did not want to miss out on fun with his "best friend."

When Dustin brought home a "B" on his report card, he could not wait to show me. I cried tears of joy. Dustin was not the only one learning, either. Seeing the positive results that Bill's loving firmness brought, I found the courage to set my own rules—and stick to them. I grew more confident in my parenting and Dustin responded well.

One day Bill asked me if it was OK for Dustin to join him for Saturday evening Mass after their afternoons out. I was amazed that Dustin had a genuine interest in attending church. As the weeks passed, I was curious about the Catholic church that they were attending. I had been a lifelong Baptist, but I started taking a Sunday morning instructional class on the Catholic faith. Dustin joined me and together we came to understand the Catholic teachings and apply them to our lives. On Easter Sunday, Dustin and I were baptized into the Catholic Church. Dustin chose Bill as his godfather. Now Dustin had both God and a father in his life.

After two years had passed, Bill had become a very important part of my son's life. When Dustin was upset or happy over something, he often called Bill. One day, Dustin was angry about something and decided that he was going to run away. I called Bill and he came over. I do not know what was said, but afterward Dustin announced that he could talk with Bill about anything. "Just like a dad, right Mom?" he said.

Bill had become central to Dustin's life, and we had gotten to know his family, too. I sometimes feared Bill would decide he had volunteered long enough. "Don't worry," Bill said one day. "I'll be here as long as Dustin needs me."

By the time Dustin was nine, all traces of his anger were gone. He was a good student and had friends. I let Bill know how much he meant to us, but he shrugged and said Dustin had just needed a friend. But it was more than just a friendship. Bill had come to represent fatherly love and security in Dustin's life .

Then, tragedy struck in Bill's life. His nineteen-year-old daughter, Malisa, was struck by a car and killed. My heart broke for this father who had given so much of himself to us. I could not imagine his pain. I expected that his grief would be too overwhelming for him to continue to keep giving to Dustin. That's when I came to understand that Bill received from Dustin as much as he gave. He asked if Dustin could sit with his family during the funeral service. I watched Dustin patting Bill's arm to comfort him. It was love and support coming full circle.

And rather than turning inward with grief, Bill found solace in reaching out. To honor the memory of his dear daughter, Bill and his wife, Becky, began a mentoring program at their church. They wanted to provide opportunities for adults to become spiritual mentors to young people. As Bill shared his vision with the congregation, I became choked up. He encouraged people to reach out to others by stating, "Dustin has brought more to my life than I ever could to his."

Dustin is seventeen years old now. He became aquainted with his father recently. The relationship grew and now Dustin lives with the father he always yearned for. But for Dustin, he has two fathers. Bill will always be a father-figure in his life. When he was twelve, he told me he wanted to grow up and be like Bill. I hope he does.

—Sharon Smith

Just Call Me "Dad"

The other day, I was speaking with an acquaintance of mine over the phone and he asked me how my life as a "househusband" was going. He didn't say this with any ill will or malice; he just really wanted to know how I was enjoying staying at home with my three-month-old son while my wife went to work as a teacher.

To my ears, however, it was as if he had just asked me how my new skirt fit or how I enjoyed my last pedicure. I imagined him laughing obnoxiously and making some obscene gestures on the other end of the line. I wanted to get in the car, drive to his office, and sock him in the mouth. That is, until he repeated in all seriousness, "So, how's it going?"

OK, I may be a tad sensitive to this staying-at-home-with-the-baby thing. A big part of the problem is that I still don't know exactly what to call myself. And believe me, when you're a dad who stays home, you find yourself constantly explaining who you are to everyone. People are fascinated by a man with a baby. Go to the grocery store on a Wednesday morning and it's "Oh, do you stay at home with the baby?" Go to the library on a weekday afternoon and the librarians start asking you about your kid in too-loud-for-the-library voices. Show up at a friend's house — someone you haven't seen since the baby was born, and it's "Did you get fired or something, man?"

So, what do I call myself? "Househusband" is definitely out. I don't need the good folks at ABC calling to cast me in their racy new spin-off series *Desperate Househusbands*. How bad does that sound? "Mr. Mom" is out, too. Too 1980s.

(I should add that the country band, Lonestar, recently cut a terrific song called "Mr. Mom." My son and I dance around his room to that sweet tune.) I don't call my working wife "Mrs. Dad," so why should I be saddled with the anachronistic "Mr. Mom?"

"Stay-at-home dad" seems to be the preferred moniker today, with "work-at-home dad" an increasingly likable option. Google the term "stay-at-home dad" and you'll find quite a bit of information, including news about the Annual At-Home Dads Convention—the ninth annual meeting was recently held in Chicago—and meetings of "dad groups" in communities across the country. You'll be pointed to neat sites like www.rebeldad.com and www.slowlane.com, both dedicated to promoting the interests of America's 190,000 stay-at-home dads.

With the work of these groups, I foresee the day when "stay-at-home dads" will supplant "soccer moms" as a parenting force—and voting bloc—to be reckoned with. Don't be surprised in 2012 to see the presidential candidates on the podiums at their respective conventions promising to stay-at-home dads from coast to coast: "I've got your back."

The only drawback with "stay-at-home dad" is that it sounds a bit like a command you'd give a dog. I envision my wife getting in the car to go to work and as she backs down the driveway, she stops, rolls down her window, points a finger at me and orders: "Stay at home, Dad. Stay. Good boy." And I turn back into the house, tail between my legs.

In my case, "work-at-home dad" sounds good, but also conveys a smidgen of self-doubt: "I do stay at home with the baby, but I work, too. Honest." Of course, when you introduce yourself as a "work-at-home dad," that inevitably leads to the question, "So, what do you do?" To which I reply,

"I'm a freelance writer." Well, I might as well say that I'm an actor, philosopher, shaman, Nintendo champion, or some other person who has more potential earning power than actual earning power. One fellow at a neighborhood block party came right out and asked, "A freelance writer? There isn't any money in that, is there?"

Well, there's no money in being an at-home dad either, but we do have one reward: a great life and an envied life. In fact, when the high school where my wife teaches high had its career day, my wife jokingly asked if I'd volunteer to come in. I'm sure the lazy boys in the back of the room would suddenly perk up, interested in how they, too, could get into this line of non-work.

I'd probably disappoint the slackers, though, when I read off the requirements for being a stay-at-home dad: must work nights, including weekends and holidays; must constantly clean up someone else's mess; must be bilingual (English and Baby Talk); and must be able to lift heavy objects, e.g., the box with disassembled crib, crates of formula, and baby in car seat. Inevitably, the kid with the green hair and "Anarkey Rulz" T-shirt would rise and ask, "Dude, we know what you do—but what do you call yourself?" And I'd say, "Just call me 'Dad.'"

—Brian Kantz

Brian Kantz is the author of "The Newbie Dad," a monthly column appearing in Buffalo's Western New York Family magazine. His column has also been read on National Public Radio's Morning Edition for member station WBFO 88.7 FM in Buffalo and has been published in regional parenting magazines in Charlotte, Tulsa, Milwaukee, and Rochester. For more information, visit Brian's website www.briankantz.com.

My Father's the Best

Our local newspaper was sponsoring an essay contest on the topic "Why My Father Is the Best." Since I was teaching a high school writing class, I chose that assignment for my class. All students but one were busily writing. Julie stared stone-faced at the wall as her pen rolled off her desk and clattered to the floor.

"Need some ideas to get started, Julie?" I prodded.

"I'm not doing this assignment!" she stated flatly. "My dad's dead."

"Is there another man you could write about then? A grandfather, maybe, or an uncle or stepfather?"

"I've had four stepfathers and they all abused me. Now my mom's new boyfriend has moved in with us." The venom in her voice made me shiver.

Not knowing how to respond, I silently pleaded with the Lord for help.

"Julie," I whispered, kneeling down beside her desk so only she could hear me. "Just because your father's dead doesn't mean you can't write about him. Pretend he's here right now. What would you tell him?"

She studied me for a few moments, then nodded. For the rest of the class, her pen scratched furiously across page after page of notebook paper. When the bell rang, Julie brought her essay to me.

"May I read it to you?" she asked quietly.

I sat down to give her my whole attention. What she read to me was a profoundly intimate love letter from a daughter to her father. Every word had been dug from the deepest level of her soul. She ended by saying, "Though you died before I could know you, you are the best father in the world. I love you, Daddy."

I've never forgotten that conversation with Julie. I, too, knew what it was like to grow up without a dad, but I never had to endure a parade of men through my home. In fact, I was so young when he died, and my mother was such a positive force in my life, that I honestly didn't feel bad about not having a father.

It wasn't until the birth of my own sons that I realized what I'd missed. One afternoon my husband, Steve, swept our son, Tyler, up in a huge bear hug and swung him around in his arms while Tyler squealed in delight.

So that's what I missed! I thought, as unexpected, jagged grief brought tears to my eyes. It was then, nearly twenty years after his death, that I began to grieve for my father. For some time, I floundered in the world of "what might have been." I began to watch hungrily the interaction between fathers and their children. The smallest act of affection—a brushed kiss, a patted hand—reduced me to tears of longing and regret. I placed pictures of my dad in various rooms around our house, even the bathroom, so I could see him wherever I was. The most often-repeated phrase in my mind became, *If only I'd had a father.*

Then a Bible verse in Romans brought my self-pity to an abrupt halt. It said we've been "adopted into the bosom of God's family" and that we call "to him 'Father, Father.' For his Holy Spirit speaks to us deep in our hearts and tells us that we really are God's children" (Rom 8:15-18, TLB).

The familiar words suddenly became rich with new meaning. *I had a father!* And He would never leave me: not through death, divorce, abuse, or abandonment ... not ever! I smiled heavenward as the security of those words wrapped around me in a warm hug.

I have a Father. And on Father's Day, He is the one I celebrate.

—Mayo Mathers

Mayo Mathers is a freelance writer, a regular contributor to Today's Christian Woman, *a former columnist for* Virtue, *and the author of two books. She travels across the United States and Canada as a conference and retreat speaker and is a speaker consultant and a member of the board of directors for Stonecroft Ministries, an international evangelistic organization. She is married to Steve, a hunting guide and outfitter and they work together in their family-owned well drilling business. They have two grown sons.*

Words of Wisdom

◈ My father used to play with my brother and me in the yard. Mother would come out and say, "You're tearing up the grass." "We're not raising grass," Dad would reply. "We're raising boys." *—Harmon Killebrew*

◈ He didn't tell me how to live; he lived, and let me watch him do it. *—Clarence Budington Kelland*

◈ A truly rich man is one whose children run into his arms when his hands are empty. *—Author Unknown*

◈ Father! — to God himself we cannot give a holier name. *—William Wordsworth*

◈ One father is more than a hundred Schoolmasters. *—George Herbert*

◈ Pray that I'll know what to say and have the courage to say it at the right time. *—Ephesians 6:19*

◈ A father delights in his son. *—Proverbs 3:12*

◈ Blessed indeed is the man who hears many gentle voices call him Father! *—Lydia M. Child*

◈ Sometimes the poorest man leaves his children the richest inheritance. *—Ruth E. Renkel*

◈ A father carries pictures where his money used to be. *—Author Unknown*

⮞ The father who would taste the essence of his fatherhood must turn back from the plane of his experience, take with him the fruits of his journey, and begin again beside his child, marching step by step over the same old road. *—Angelo Patri*

⮞ The words that a father speaks to his children in the privacy of home are not heard by the world, but, as in whispering-galleries, they are clearly heard at the end and by posterity. *—Jean Paul Richter*

⮞ Sherman made the terrible discovery that men make about their fathers sooner or later ... that the man before him was not an aging father but a boy, a boy much like himself, a boy who grew up and had a child of his own and, as best he could, out of a sense of duty and, perhaps love, adopted a role called Being a Father so that his child would have something mythical and infinitely important: a Protector, who would keep a lid on all the chaotic and catastrophic possibilities of life. *—Tom Wolfe*

⮞ Why are men reluctant to become fathers? They aren't through being children. *—Cindy Garner*

⮞ There are three stages of a man's life: He believes in Santa Claus; he doesn't believe in Santa Claus; he is Santa Claus. *—Author Unknown*

⮞ Fatherhood is pretending the present you love most is soap-on-a-rope. *—Bill Cosby*

⮞ When I was a boy of fourteen, my father was so ignorant I could hardly stand to have the old man around. But when I got to be 21, I was astonished at how much he had learned in seven years. *—Mark Twain*

– You don't really understand human nature unless you know why a child on a merry-go-round will wave at his parents every time around—and why his parents will always wave back. *—William D. Tammeus*

– Always kiss your children goodnight—even if they're already asleep. *—H. Jackson Brown, Jr.*

– Parenthood: That state of being better chaperoned than you were before marriage. *—Marcelene Cox*

– Before I got married I had six theories about bringing up children; now I have six children, and no theories. *—John Wilmot*

– To bring up a child in the way he should go, travel that way yourself once in a while. *—Josh Billings*

– Don't worry that children never listen to you; worry that they are always watching you. *—Robert Fulghum*

– Parents often talk about the younger generation as if they didn't have anything to do with it. *—Haim Ginott*

– It behooves a father to be blameless if he expects his child to be. *—Homer*

– Most of us become parents long before we have stopped being children. *—Mignon McLaughlin*

X X X X ✎ Don't handicap your children by making their lives
easy. *—Robert A. Heinlein*

✎ Too often we give children answers to remember rather
than problems to solve. *—Roger Lewin*

✎ There are two lasting bequests we can give our children.
One is roots. The other is wings. *—Hodding Carter, Jr.*

✎ The thing that impresses me most about America is the
way parents obey their children.
—Edward, Duke of Windsor

✎ Each day of our lives we make deposits in the memory
banks of our children. *—Charles R. Swindoll*

✎ You will always be your child's favorite toy.
—Vicki Lansky

✎ What a child doesn't receive he can seldom later give.
—P.D. James

✎ If you want your children to improve, let them overhear
the nice things you say about them to others.
—Haim Ginott

✎ Give me the life of the boy whose mother is nurse,
seamstress, washerwoman, cook, teacher, angel, and
saint, all in one, and whose father is guide, exemplar,
and friend. No servants to come between. These are
the boys who are born to the best fortune.
—Andrew Carnegie

ᦥ Kids spell love T-I-M-E. —*John Crudele*

ᦥ A parent who has never apologized to his children is a monster. If he's *always* apologizing, his children are monsters. —*Mignon McLaughlin*

ᦥ The most important thing a father can do for his children is to love their mother. —*Henry Ward Beecher*

ᦥ One night a father overheard his son pray, "Dear God, make me the kind of man my Daddy is." Later that night, the father prayed, "Dear God, make me the kind of man my son wants me to be." —*Anonymous*

Catch and Release

An old hurt lay buried between father and son, watered with silence, fertilized by time. It grew strong, as such hurts do when left neglected by forgiveness.

Sarah warily watched it grow between her husband and his father. She was there when it was planted and continually sought a way to uproot the ugly old thing.

The only balm she had found so far was Joshua, her son. Each man showed the child unrestrained love—as if the feelings they used to have for each other needed an outlet, a beneficiary, an heir.

Joshua loved Grandpa Bill and his stories of growing up way back in the woods. And for two weeks every summer, Sarah would take Joshua to Grandpa's house by the lake.

There on the dock, Grandpa Bill and Joshua would sit, fishing from sun-up until she called them in for supper. Yet Sarah never let Joshua go out in the boat—he was too little, she'd say.

One summer, after Grandpa Bill and Joshua pleaded and pleaded, Sarah finally agreed to let the boy go out on the boat. The one condition Sarah set was that Joshua would have to wait until after his seventh birthday, which was later that month.

Sarah's husband, Ted, never came along on the visits to his father's house. But Sarah insisted Joshua get to know his grandpa, for Sarah regretted never knowing her own grandparents.

For Joshua's birthday, Ted gave him his first fishing pole. It was just a lightweight rod with a foolproof reel, but Joshua couldn't wait to go out on Grandpa Bill's lake.

Before the birthday dishes were done, Sarah had called Grandpa Bill and arranged for Joshua to go out in the boat. When Ted found out he was furious.

"It's the boy's first fishing trip, Sarah, and I wanted to take him out myself," Ted said.

"Then go with them," Sarah said, as she dried the last of the dishes.

"You know that's not possible," Ted replied flatly.

Sarah threw down her dishtowel and turned on Ted. Glowering she said, "I know no such thing, Ted Wilkins! All I know is that Joshua wants nothing more than to go fishing with his grandpa and his father. What kind of man are you to let an old argument stop you from making your son happy?"

Ted's indignation deflated before Sarah's logic. She had a point and it struck him to the heart.

"Well, he won't let me on his property, let alone in the boat," Ted said under his breath, as he turned away.

"He will after I'm through with him!" Sarah replied as she headed for the phone.

It was a long conversation, but a fruitful one, as Grandpa Bill reluctantly agreed to let Ted join their party.

∽

Their greeting, after so many years, was cool and conducted under the watchful eye of Sarah—but one look at Joshua's face set both men in their place. The boy was positively glowing. This had been his secret birthday wish.

They loaded the boat with enough fishing gear to sink the Titanic, as each man took his own tackle box of secrets. Sarah securely wrapped Joshua in a bright orange life vest, which came all the way up to his nose when he sat down in the wide aluminum boat.

As Sarah released the bowline and pushed the boat away from the dock, Ted and Grandpa Bill called out "Aren't you coming along?"

"No, fishing is a guy thing," she replied, as she waved them off. "Have fun!"

Ted sat in the bow stubbornly facing due starboard, with Joshua in the broad middle seat by the rods. Grandpa Bill ran the outboard, looking everywhere but at the bow.

Each man took turns showing Joshua how to spinner fish for walleye, how to troll for trout, how to work a bass plug. But never once did either man speak to the other—only to Joshua.

They tried the rock banks, the deep shaded pools, the underwater shelves, even along the sheer granite wall. But after a full day they were snookered: not one fish among them. Finally, they tried floating worms off the bottom near the reed-choked sandbar.

"This isn't what I thought it would be like," Joshua pouted, as they sat rocking in silence. He could sense the tension between his father and his grandpa, but he didn't understand it.

"Well, Joshua, some days are like this," Ted explained.

Just then, Joshua's line took off—in an instant both men were talking to him.

"Keep your pole up!" Grandpa shouted excitedly.

"Reel, son, reel!" Ted said, with equal enthusiasm. "Check your drag."

Joshua didn't have a clue what that meant; he'd never really caught anything big enough to take out much line.

"Dad, reach over and check his drag; he doesn't know how," Ted quickly added.

The fish paused in his battle for freedom and Grandpa Bill reached over the struggling boy's hands. With practiced skill, he took the line between his forefinger and thumb; one tug told him the drag was way too tight.

The old trout was not tiring; in fact, he had other ideas. Angrily, he rose to the surface, jumping into the hot summer air some forty feet from the boat. He flashed a rainbow of silver and green as the water flipped from his powerful body.

Then came the sound both men knew meant disaster— the twanging sorrow of line separating under too much strain.

Grandpa Bill still had a tentative hold on the line between his fingers, but not for long.

"Grab the line up the pole, Ted," he shouted.

Ted dove for the rendered line whipping through the pole guides.

Joshua fell backward into the bottom of the boat, as the tension on the pole suddenly ceased. Grandpa Bill grabbed the monofilament line and began hauling it in hand over fist.

Bill took in as much line as he could before getting his hands caught up in knots, then Ted would take over, until he, too, was entangled. By then his father would be free to take over once more. Palms were cut and fingers sliced by the struggling line, yet each man continued without complaint, for it was Joshua's first fish.

"I see him! Get the net, Joshua; get the net!" Ted hollered.

Joshua reached over the tipping boat's side and scooped the bright green net under the trout. But the fish was not done just yet.

With a powerful thrust of his tail, he jumped three feet straight up. Thinking fast, Joshua stood on his seat and swirled the net after him, catching the fish mid-air like a butterfly.

Together, Ted and Bill grabbed Joshua's life vest, hauling the boy down to safety.

The two men and the boy laughed hysterically as a five-pound trout slimed the bottom of the boat. Joshua had caught his first fish—and set more than the boat to rights.

All the way home, the three relived their part in the triumph like old friends.

Sarah was absolutely amazed when they neared the dock, for each of them vied to recount the story. The cold distant manner was gone from their voices, as each man cut into the story to compliment the other for some daring act in the tale while Joshua, his chest lifted with pride, held the stringer with one single, but very important, fish.

Sarah took a photo of the three of them, arms about each other, with Joshua and his fish in the middle. All were grinning like they had caught the biggest fish in the world.

"Hey, Dad, let's go show him how to clean it," Ted said, as they headed for the dock.

As they walked away, Sarah smiled to herself. All it had taken was one boy and one fish to make them a family again.

—Dee Berry

Dee Berry currently pursues her passions for writing, fishing, and gardening in Washington State. She would like to thank her dad for teaching her to sit still long enough to catch something. That lesson has served her well in life. She can be reached at DeeBerryWrites@hotmail.com.

Dad on Defense

"Whatever you do, don't ask him to pass anything."

Teach Your Children

On one of my first trips to Israel, I was eager to see and experience all that I could of its land, people, and customs after studying the Jewish roots of the Christian faith. As I found myself in Jerusalem at the base of the Temple Mount, I could sense the fervor of Jewish worshippers coming in contact with God as close as they could venture to the holy spot of their Temple, which was destroyed nearly 2,000 years ago. The large plaza where men assemble to pray touches the Western Wall of the Temple Mount. The men, heads covered and prayer shawls spread across their shoulders, pray along the wall to the north and the women to the south.

I wanted to be part—in some way—of the men praying in the partitioned area. I was handed a white cardboard cap, or *kipa* as it is called in Hebrew. Balancing it onto my head, I stepped into the moving mass of men and boys rocking back and forth in prayer, many of them wrapped with phylacteries, the leather straps upon their left arms and foreheads. These leather boxes contain the verses from the Old Testament instructing the Hebrews to bind the word of God to their hearts and minds. At the corner of the plaza is part of an arch that led to a room filled with more men and boys. Intrigued, I wove my way through the worshippers to peer in. There I saw the back of a seated man whose prayer shawl was larger than any I had seen and whose head moved from one side to the other. "What could he possibly be doing?" I wondered, and skirted around him to take a look at the front of him.

To my amazement, beneath this large black and white prayer shawl, two boys perched on their father's knees. The boys were holding open the Scriptures and the father first leaned his head to one son and instructed him and then leaned to the other and instructed him. The little boys with their side curls dangling from their temples listened intently while their father taught them.

What a lesson for me, a new father, at the sight of this man so diligently teaching his sons the Scriptures. I could tell that in their home, the Scriptures weren't something mentioned or hinted at on occasion. In that man's house, the children knew the Scriptures and their lessons. This man was investing his life and time into his sons to be sure the faith was passed to them. He was a visual reminder of what Moses told Israel in Deuteronomy 6:6-9: "And these words which I command you this day shall be upon your heart; and you shall teach them diligently to your children, and shall talk of them when you sit in your house, and when you walk by the way and when you lie down, and when you rise. And you shall bind them as a sign upon your hand, and they shall be as frontlets between your eyes. And you shall write them on the doorposts of your house and on your gates." As is often the case in Israel, a picture is worth a thousand words.

—Jeff Cavins

Jeff Cavins is the co-creator and an editor of the Amazing Grace series. His biography appears at the end of the book.

God Among the Winos

When my daughter, Holly, was four, she made a man visible just by talking to him. The two of us had been walking down an uncrowded street together and I could have sworn there wasn't another soul within fifty yards of us. But suddenly I heard her say "Hi." The sound of her voice and a slight tug from her hand stopped me in my tracks. I had seen no one.

I turned and saw Holly gazing up into the bleary eyes of an old wino. I wondered where he had come from. "Well, hello there," he said—to Holly, not me. The clothes he was wearing looked like he hadn't taken them off for a week or more. He was unshaven and the smell of fortified wine clung to him. He looked surprised, delighted, and maybe a little stunned that my daughter had not only seen him but had felt an urge to greet him.

I was embarrassed. Holly and I had encountered another human being on the street and I hadn't even seen him. The whole episode made me uncomfortable. I made my living as a journalist. If I couldn't trust my own senses, how much credibility could I rightfully claim? The man was obviously a skid row derelict, but was he such an insignificant lump of humanity that I could pass him on the street and not even see him? I felt guilty.

We are all God's children, I told myself as I looked lovingly at Holly. Even the winos.

Especially the winos. That last thought sort of injected itself into my mind. I tried to make it go away because it was illogical and discomforting. As far as I was concerned, God didn't play favorites.

A few days later I was covering a lecture by Mother Teresa in Boston and something she said particularly grabbed my attention. The poorest of the poor, she told us, the wretched of the earth, the dying beggars covered with lice and scabs, are God Himself. Jesus, she said, comes to us in terrible disguises to see if we love Him.

It was a beautiful thought, but it was too challenging. I couldn't imagine myself tending to the needs of dying beggars, bathing their wounds, and comforting them for hours on end the way Mother Teresa's Missionaries of Charity do.

A few evenings later, after dark, I was leaving my office when a drunk accosted me. "Did the bus leave yet?" he asked. He reminded me of the guy Holly had spoken to but he he was even dirtier.

"The bus doesn't stop here," I told him.

"The sisters' bus," he insisted. Then I understood. I vaguely remembered evenings when a van from a soup kitchen stopped here to pick up street people, but he had missed it. Suddenly, it dawned on me that I should give him a ride.

I didn't really buy the idea that this old bum was God in disguise, but I could see a person in front of me and he needed a meal. All I had to do was offer him a ride. The soup kitchen wasn't very far out of my way. I could do that much. I just hoped he wouldn't throw up in the car.

"I think the bus left already, but I'll drive you."

He looked surprised, delighted, and a little stunned. He studied me with bleary eyes. His next words floated to me on the smell of cheap wine but I'll never forget them.

"Say, you must know me."

Mother Teresa's words were realized in my life that very day: "Jesus comes to us in terrible disguises to see if we love Him."

—Bob Baldwin

For many years Bob Baldwin worked as a writer and editor for secular and religious publications, and he traveled as far as Israel, Cambodia, Yugoslavia, and Haiti for stories. Today, he writes books and songs, visits schools, and tells stories for kids that show them how science, poetry, and natural beauty are connected. Of all his work, he is proudest of This is the Sea that Feeds Us, *which won a Teachers' Choice award.*

Whispered Prayers

I lie in bed thinking of all the memories these walls hold. I'm visiting my parents, sleeping in my old room, and remembering my last night thirty years ago when I left home to become a sister in a religious order. I thought then that nothing would ever be the same. Next time I returned, I thought that things would be different at home and I would be different. It's true. However, one thing has remained constant. As I lie in bed I hear the "psst psst psst" whispers of my father's prayers. My father's night prayers have been holding up the sky for as long as I can remember. I have memories as a small child of running into my parents' room and finding my father kneeling at his bedside saying his night prayers. I've noticed in recent years that my father now has his own altar. I think it has been there for years but I had never noticed it. It is not like my mother's *altarcito* with little statues and candles, pictures, and mementos. His altar is simply a framed picture of Jesus. He stands before it with his arms folded across his chest. I recognize that stance. That is how I imagine the ancient Aztecs standing before their gods. Each night my father assumes his prayer stance and whispers to God his gratitude along with his concerns and petitions for each of us, his children and grandchildren, and for the world. I fall asleep comforted by the "psst, psst, psst" of my father's prayers and secure that all will be well with the world.

I often ask the students in my prayer and spirituality classes to talk about their spiritual models or mentors. Invariably, they will talk about their mothers or grandmothers. Very rarely does anyone think of or describe his or her father as a spiritual role model. Is it that men are not considered spiritually oriented? Do we deny, overlook, or not recognize the ways that men express their spirituality? Do men themselves try to mask or hide their religious piety? Some in our society still believe "boys don't cry." Do boys not express their spirituality openly either? I realize that I risk embarrassing my father with this description of his personal piety. It is not insignificant that he prays late at night when he assumes all of us are asleep and out of hearing range. His altar is in the same room where I watch television when I am home. I notice he starts getting restless when he is ready to retire and I am still in there. I know it's his prayer time and that he needs his privacy, so I yawn and announce my departure.

I don't really feel qualified to probe further into men's spirituality, but I can comment on my experience of growing up seeing my father pray. I believe that I got the message early in my life that we depend on God for everything. If my father, whom I believed could do anything, got on his knees every night and prayed, then surely God must be powerful. Like most children, I think that it was not until I left home and became an adult that I really came to appreciate the impact of the rich Latino Catholic environment that I grew up in. My parents' praying, the religious images throughout our house, the nightly benediction that we received from each of our parents before bed, the prayers we said together around the table, the family rosary, all contributed to a tangible sense of God's presence. From the earliest memories of my father praying by his bedside at night to the present, I know that my parents' prayers carry me through the day.

In my family there were seven children. During that period, when we were all still pretty young and rowdy, my parents would take turns going to Mass on Sundays. My father always went to Mass at 6:00 a.m. and, against my mother's objections, returned with a big bag of sugar-coated sweetbread from the Mexican bakery. We would eagerly await his return from church. As we got older we all went to Sunday Mass together, not necessarily in perfect harmony. In those times of one-bathroom houses someone had always stayed in the bathroom too long and made someone else late. As we got older and each went our own way, my parents would have everyone over for *menudo*, a Mexican soup, on Sunday mornings and quiz us about the Sunday readings at Mass. Often, when I call home on Sunday afternoons, my father will still get on the phone to ask me if I've already been to Mass. On those occasions when I have not been to Mass yet, I'm sure glad for the Sunday evening liturgy schedule in my parish.

Apart from times of private prayer and formal religious observance, my father's spirituality is most visible on the canvas of daily life. He is never too tired to comfort a grandchild or to run an errand for my mother, or to be present to us when we need him. Now that he is retired he has more time for "the things that really count," spending more time with each of us and with God. In 1 Corinthians 13, love is described as being patient and kind; there is no limit to its forbearance, its trust, its hope, its power to endure. That description fits my experience of my father. It is the legacy that he has given me and that will live on in the expression of my spirituality.

When I think of spiritual mentors or guides, I think of those people who both exhibit a deep spirituality and inspire us to seek that same "pearl of great price." I realize now that my father was one of my first spiritual mentors. By his example, he taught me that we depend on God for our very life and that our life is for bringing the experience of God's love to others.

—Sr. Yolanda Tarango, CCVI

Sister Yolanda Tarango, CCVI, D.Min., is the co-founder and current director of Visitation House, a transitional housing program for homeless women and children in San Antonio, Texas. An author and lecturer on issues of importance to Latina women, she has served as national coordinator of Las Hermanas, a national Latina organization, and is a fellow of the National Hispana Leadership Institute. Sister Yolanda has served on the central leadership team of the Sisters of Charity of the Incarnate Word and currently teaches in the religious studies department of the University of the Incarnate Word.

A Second Fatherhood

In order to for me to answer God's call to the fullness of my fatherhood, I first had to experience my deepest sorrow. As a happily married father of three grown children, the loss of my dear wife of thirty-seven years left a painful hole in my life. Norah slipped away after suffering for seven years with lymphoma. When her breathing stopped, a light suddenly went out. But in the midst of my darkest hour, I felt Christ calling me to another life: that of the priesthood.

During Norah's long illness, we began to talk about about whether I should actually move forward in my pursuit of the priesthood after her death. We both believed that God had plans for me. Now, instead of being a father to three children, I became a father to many. Instead of ministering to people's physical needs as a doctor of forty years, I would minister to their spiritual needs. I looked forward to the next stage of my life journey, but I would never stop missing Norah.

We met in 1949 when I was an intern. I quickly became smitten with Norah Muldoon, who was a young surgical nurse. Eleven months later, we were married. During our first five years of marriage, I experienced the profound joy of fatherhood three times with the births of Tim, Sheila, and Kevin. I took to fatherhood easily. To me, the life of my children was a miraculous extension of my love for Norah and the fruits of our marriage.

During the early years of our marriage, from 1951 to 1961, I worked in the anesthesiology departments of Air Force hospitals in Texas and Germany. I often reflected on all my blessings. I had achieved my childhood ambition of becoming a doctor and had a loving marriage with three beautiful children. It seemed I lacked for nothing.

Then, one Saturday in June of 1956, I learned that my fatherhood was not fully complete. I was stationed in Germany with my family. Norah and I were preparing lunch together in the kitchen, listening to news on the radio. There was a report that the Catholic Church was considering a married priesthood since clerical celibacy is a discipline rather than an unchangeable doctrine. Never before had I even considered such a vocation. Norah and I suddenly looked at each other and said simultaneously that I should look into that. In that instant, we both knew that one day I would become a priest. At the time, I was thirty years old, married, and the father of three young children. For a variety of reasons, the Church concluded that a married clergy would not be right for the universal church, with limited exceptions. Yet, from that day forward, we knew with certainty that I had been called. It was never really discussed after that, but there was an understanding between us. For the next thirty years, we lived life as a normal Catholic family—doing our best to live the faith ourselves and raise our children in the Lord.

Then, one day, Norah had something to tell me. "Dick," she began, "I made a request of God. I knew it would be OK with you."

Norah and I both had strong spiritual lives, so I assumed that any deal Norah made with God would be fine with me. But this one took me by surprise. It concerned a friend of ours who had cancer and was not expected to live through the year. She was the mother of three young boys. Norah looked me square in the eyes and very matter-of-factly explained, "I asked God to give me cancer in return for letting her live long enough to raise her boys."

I took a deep breath. We had a good life together; I envisioned an equally happy retirement one day. But Norah knew me well. She knew I would never deny God or her anything. Our own children were in college at that time and very independent. Never had I loved or respected Norah more than at that moment. Her capacity to love was boundless. As John 15:13 tells us, "Greater love has no man than this, that a man lay down his life for his friends."

With tears in my eyes, I hugged Norah. "Yes," I said softly. "It's OK with me."

Our friend lived until her youngest child was in high school. Then, a couple of years later in 1980, Norah went to the doctor's for a lump on her stomach. A biopsy revealed it to be an untreatable but slow growing cancer of the lymph glands.

Norah fought for her life for seven years and I prayed for more time with her. But in the end, we accepted God's will. We thought back to that afternoon in 1956 when we believed God had called me to the priesthood. On our thirty-seventh wedding anniversary, Norah took a turn for the worse. She would live only another six months. During that time, our children learned of my call to the priesthood. It was Norah who told them one by one. She wanted to prepare our children for their Dad's new spouse—the Catholic Church.

Each of the kids had the same reaction: "What? What are you saying?"

Norah would explain, "Daddy got a call many years ago. We've known that I would one day die because he's going to become a priest. "

At first, I think they were all so shocked. No one said much about it. But as it became obvious Norah's time was almost up, we started talking about it together with her there. Sheila and Kevin were both in medical school and

Tim was studying to be a Jesuit priest, although he would eventually discern that he was called to the married life.

The children were mourning the impending loss of their mother, and now they feared they would lose me, too. I reassured them that I would always be their loving father. Gradually, any resistance faded and the idea took hold. By the time Norah passed away, all three kids were behind me.

In spite of the inner certainty of my call to the priesthood, I recognized I was human. Just as Jesus wept at the tomb of Lazarus, even knowing He would raise him in just a few minutes, I wept each day for the loss of Norah. Still, I also rejoiced for her, knowing that eye has not seen and ear has not heard what God has prepared for those who love Him.

I waited a few months to give myself time to mourn. Then, one morning, I made a visit to the director of vocations for the Archdioces of Seattle. No doubt, he assumed I was making a social call. When I revealed my real purpose—that I was presenting myself for the priesthood—his face fell. Perhaps he imagined I was suffering from some sort of post-grief delirium.

In his defense, the director had good cause for doubting my rationality. I was a full professor and well known in the field of anesthesia. Becoming a priest would mean walking away from it all: my forty-year medical career, my faculty position, my beautiful home, a collection of antique furniture and sports cars, and all the other trappings. To top it off, I was sixty-two years old. The director had never encountered such a situation before. But I was adamant. "God has called me to be a priest," I had to tell him more than once.

After completing four years of theology studies in three-and-a-half years, I was ordained in 1993 by Archbishop Thomas J. Murphy of Seattle alongside another widower and grandfather. The first several rows were filled with both our children and grandchildren and I know our two wives were there in spirit. On that day, it seemed there was not a dry eye in the church, including mine. I felt humbled before God, that He had chosen me for so great a mission. My own fatherhood had been such a blessing, and now, my children would extend to all of the Church.

Through the priesthood, I received an infusion of grace to love and shepherd all my children, not just those who had been born to me. My own children learned that our relationship did not diminish though my priesthood. Instead, God have me a supernatural ability to father. The penitents who came to me in confession were my children, seeking guidance and God's forgiveness. At Mass, my homilies were expanded versions of fatherly advice a man gives his children. And just as a father provides for his chiildren, I became a father blessed with the ability to feed my children with the Holy Eucharist—to fill them spiritually with the Bread of Life.

My humble fatherhood had been lifted to the divine. And yet, my simple beginnings as a dad who slugged his way through everything from teething and toddlerhood to adolescence and an empty nest, often drew people to me. When they learned I had been both a father and a doctor, I frequently felt people open up to me; I could relate to them on many levels. As a doctor, I could understand people's illnesses, and then minister to their souls. Having been married, people often approached me on issues of sexuality. I was able to understand their issues or confusion and yet hold firm to Church teaching. And as a father, I knew the love of a child. God allowed my fatherly love to grow. Now, I served as a representative of Christ—a father to all his children.

—Fr. Dick Ward

Fr. Dick Ward served as a priest for ten years in the Archdiocese of Seattle. At the age of 81, Fr. Ward is retired, if you can call it that. He averages four Masses a week, filling in for other priests and doing funerals. He now enjoys spending time with his four grandchildren.

Blue Ribbon

A teacher in New York decided to honor each of her high school seniors for the difference they made in her life. Then she presented each of them with a Blue Ribbon imprinted with gold letters that read, "Who I Am Makes a Difference."

Afterward, the teacher gave each of the students three more ribbons to pass on and acknowledge others, to see what impact it would have in their community. They were to follow up on the results, see who honored whom, and report back to the class the following week.

One of the students honored a junior executive in a nearby company for helping him with his career planning. The student gave him a blue ribbon and put it on his shirt just over his heart. Then the boy gave him two extra ribbons, explained their class project on acknowledgement and enlisted the executive's help.

Later that day the junior executive went in to his boss and told him that he deeply admired him for being a creative genius. The junior executive asked him if he would accept the gift of the blue ribbon and would he give him permission to put it on him. His surprised boss said, "Well, sure." After placing the ribbon above his boss' heart, he asked him to support the efforts of the class project and pass on the last ribbon.

That night the boss went home to his fourteen-year-old son and sat him down. He said, "The most incredible thing happened to me today. I was in my office and one of the junior executives came in and told me he admired me and gave me this blue ribbon for being a creative genius. Imagine.

He thinks I'm a creative genius. Then he put this blue ribbon that says 'Who I Am Makes a Difference'® on my jacket above my heart. Next he gave me an extra ribbon and asked me to find somebody else to honor. As I was driving home tonight, I started thinking about whom I would honor with this ribbon and I thought about you, son. I want to honor you."

"My days are really hectic, and when I come home I don't pay a lot of attention to you. Sometimes I scream at you for not getting good enough grades in school or for your bedroom being a mess. But somehow tonight, I just wanted to sit here and just let you know that you do make a difference to me. Besides your mother, you are the most important person in my life. You're a great kid and I love you!"

The startled boy started to sob and sob, and he couldn't stop crying. His whole body shook. He walked over to a drawer, pulled out a gun, stared at his father and, through his tears said, "I was planning on committing suicide tomorrow, Dad, because I didn't think you loved me. Now I don't need to."

—Helice "Sparky" Bridges

Helice "Sparky" Bridges is the founder of Difference Makers International and the inventor of the "Who I Am Makes A Difference" Blue Ribbon and 8-Step Ceremony. She delivers this powerful message at conferences, corporations, schools, organizations and churches throughout the world. Helice is the recipient of the prestigious 2005 Gandhi Nonviolence Award. Her stories appear in the Chicken Soup for the Soul *book series. Visit* www.blueribbons.org *for more information.*

Dad's Gift

My dad has always been a natural teacher, so it wasn't surprising that someone at the parish would put "the arm" on him to teach religious education. One September, many years ago, a nun called and asked if he would take over a class of eighth-grade boys.

Dad threw himself into the challenge with enthusiasm. He would prepare his lessons with ingenuity and care, constantly dreaming up ways to entice the dry bones of eternal truths to come to life in the hearts and imaginations of his charges.

I was proud of my father and his flair for teaching. Yet I couldn't understand why he had agreed to teach eighth grade CCD. I was in sixth grade at the Catholic school, but I knew all about those public school eighth graders: they smoked, they spit, they swore, they talked dirty to the girls, and they wore their hair slicked back like James Dean.

I took it upon myself to let Dad know what kind of boys he would be dealing with, but he wouldn't listen. He was clearly enjoying teaching these boys religion, much to my eleven-year-old surprise. As the weeks went along, I looked for signs of disaffection on Dad's part, but I saw none. If anything, he grew more enthused about his class by the week.

Just before Christmas, a food drive was launched in the religious education program. Someone decided that gathering food and bringing it to the poor would be a good way to teach the students how to put their faith into action.

My young mind figured the effort would flop, given the nature of the kids, but each week Dad reported how the jumbo collection boxes were filling up with stockpiles of canned goods and toys. Still, something seemed fishy to me. "How could public school kids be as generous as those of us who went to Catholic school every day?" I wondered.

We were scheduled to deliver the food on the Saturday before Christmas. Dad made it clear that I was to help, even though I wasn't even in his class. That day was also the first winter snowfall in Chicago. Big thick flakes floated oh-so-lazily from a low gray sky, covering our neighborhood in an inviting blanket of white.

My friends, I knew, would be trudging up and down the block, towing their sleds and looking for me, but I had to go out with a bunch of juvenile delinquents and deliver Christmas baskets. I waited in the steamy heat of our kitchen for Dad to get home from work, watching the snow begin to fall in earnest. He bustled in, shoulders full of snow, a smile on his face. His hand was cold on my forehead as he tousled my hair and asked if I was ready. Clearly, I was not as ready as he was.

At the parish parking lot, most of the teachers and students had gathered and were loaded into cars. Seven of the eighth-grade guys jammed into the back of our car, squeezing me into a tight space over the hump in the back seat. Dad's '54 Ford was a tank with no ventilation, and I felt smothered by wet wool and the breath of guys who'd spent their morning standing around smoking.

We pulled up at our first stop—not a parish, which I guess is what I had expected, but an apartment building. We all got out of the car, opened the trunk, and stood around embarrassed and uncertain what to do next. Dad quickly took over and led the charge. He gave us each something to carry and we made our way to the first address on his list. An old woman opened the door a crack. She was frightened and suspicious, even when Dad laid on the old Irish charm. He understood why she might be uncomfortable, and we left the food on the landing outside her doorway, wished her Merry Christmas, and thumped our way back down the stairs. As we got to the bottom landing, we heard her rummaging through the bags. And then she yelled from above, "God bless you! God bless you boys!"

At the next stop we met a tired young mother with a bunch of kids who were running wild through the apartment. It wasn't clear whether these were all her children. She showed no emotion when we arrived, seemingly resigned to whatever twists and turns life would send her next. We all stood at the door feeling awkward, but then Dad got her talking. Yes, she knew Father McGinty from the local parish. "Oh, he gave you my name? Well, would you like to come in and have a cup of coffee? I think I have some cookies around here someplace for the boys."

So we brought in the bags and boxes. I noticed that Dad's students were uncommonly subdued. There was no flash, no swagger, no attitude. One of the kids from the house, a little boy about five, stood face to face with Stuart, the leader of Dad's pack of hoodlums. The little boy stood stone still for some time and then—moved by some primordial urge—flung his metal toy truck right at Stuart's head. I gasped, figuring the kid was in for it now. A sneer did cross Stuart's face, but then the look passed. He knelt down and got eye level with the kid. He smiled and said, "Some kinda arm you got there. You like baseball?"

And then Stuart reached into the shopping bag he had been carrying and took out a rubber ball. "Here," he said. "This is for you."

The boy grabbed the ball, hugged it with both hands to his chest, and did a little dance of joy. We all laughed—Dad, his gang of ne'r-do-wells, and me—and the mother and the other children in the family laughed, too. We boys spent a little time showing the kids their new toys and playing with them while Dad had a cup of coffee with the lady. They were visiting as if they were long lost family members.

We finally left the family and then stopped at three other homes, each time meeting people we never expected to meet—recent immigrants, people in "broken homes," people I'd looked down on from the "el" as we rode by on our way. We went into neighborhoods I had always passed through in fear, breathing easier only when we got to our familiar turf again.

When we pulled up at our last stop, snow was continuing to fall unabated. The other boys and I milled around the back of the car. They were beginning to include me in their number. Down the block a menacing looking group of men were standing around some double-parked cars. One of the men got the attention of his companion and nodded toward our crowd. I got scared, then I heard a shout.

Dad looked up, and the smile broadened into a boyish grin. "Holy smokes!" he cried. "If it isn't 'The Professor' himself." (Dad had nicknames for everybody.) He left us standing there and walked toward the men. Soon there were handshakes and shoulder slaps and smiles all around. One of the men worked with Dad, and Dad soon called us over and introduced us.

One of the cars the men had been working on had a bad ignition switch. They were about to maneuver it out into the street and push it to a running start, so all of us boys joined in this exciting—but foolhardy—effort. Slipping and sliding along the street, we got the car moving at a decent clip and the guy behind the wheel popped the clutch and the motor turned over. The man waved wildly out the driver-side window, fishtailing his way down the street, and one of the guys called out something in Spanish and the men all laughed. My dad asked what they'd said and his co-worker explained, "He told the guy, 'Don't stop until you get to Guadalajara!'"

After that, the men brought out beer and soda and we all stood around having a drink. It no longer seemed cold. Kids from the neighborhood came by and we chatted.

When it was time to get going, Dad asked his friend if he knew the family we were supposed to deliver to next. He did; they were related to his wife. Dad said, "Could you do us a favor? I've got something that belongs to them. Could you make sure they get it? Just some stuff for Christmas."

"I will," the man said. "We're bringing them a ham later today anyway."

When we piled back into the car, the guys laid me across their lap and teased me about being so small. I laughed along with them. I even cracked a few jokes and got them laughing. I began to see them as their family members probably saw them—as goofy but good boys. When we got back to the parish parking lot it felt good to be out in the open air again. The guys stood around, no one wanting to leave. We stood for a few minutes looking at each other as snow piled up on our heads and shoulders.

Finally, the boys all shook my dad's hand and wished him a Merry Christmas. Then they shook mine, too. Dad reminded them he'd like to see them at Mass Christmas morning. "We'll see about that, Mr. McGrath," they said and laughed, but somehow I got the feeling that we might just see them there.

"Thanks for taking us today," said Stuart, speaking for the gang. "It wasn't stupid like we thought it would be."

"No," said Dad. "It wasn't stupid at all."

When Dad and I got home, the Christmas tree lights were on and the house smelled of dinner on the stove. Mom had me slip into warm jeans and a flannel shirt fresh from the dryer. Dickens' *A Christmas Carol*—the good one with Alistair Sims—was on TV. I sat on the couch feeling surprisingly full, since I hadn't eaten since breakfast. I had been out in the world, and now I was home. Only now, my heart was bigger and I was ready for Christmas.

Years before that Christmas, when my Dad would come home from work in the summer, all the little kids in the neighborhood—Steve and Jan and Jeffery and Susie and everybody—would run madly down the street and into his arms. He would swoop them up and hold them high above his head and call them by name.

The day we delivered Christmas presents to the poor, I finally realized that what Dad was doing each week with his religious education class was swooping the boys up and holding them high and calling them by name—just as he always did with me.

That has always been his gift.

—Tom McGrath

Tom McGrath is vice president of new product development at Loyola Press and the author of Raising Faith-Filled Kids: Ordinary Opportunities to Nurture Spirituality at Home. *Tom, his wife, and their two grown daughters, Patti and Judy, reside in Chicago.*

Chapter 7
A Father's Hope

The Baseball Sign

Nothing could have prepared me for the moment I walked into my son's hospital room. As a veteran of the Boston Police Department, I had seen it all—except for this. This was my first-born, my namesake, my very own son. Dennis, at twenty, lay in a coma after an alleged drunken driver collided with his car. Surrounded by tubes and machines, he could not even breathe on his own.

Dennis had been training with the U.S. Air Force in Florida and had been visiting friends in Mississippi. It was one of his friends who had called to tell us that there had been a terrible accident. My wife, Maureen, and I had called the hospital but they would not give us details over the phone. Maureen stayed with our two other children, Danielle, eighteen, and David, fourteen, while I hopped on the first flight to Mississippi.

At the hospital, a doctor met with me before taking me to Dennis's room. "He is in a coma," he reported solemnly. "It's possible Dennis could come out of it and be fine. He could come out of it and suffer brain damage. Or, he could die. Only time will tell."

I hung on to the first possibility. "Dear God, let my son be all right," I prayed. I looked at my boy, lying perfectly still. "Dennis, I'm here," I whispered. "I love you. You are going to get better." I stayed by his side for around half an hour and quitely prayed out loud; then I went down to the hospital chapel. On my knees, I broke down for the first time. As a police officer, I had learned to steel myself against life's hard realities. I was tough, not given to emotion. But before God, the tears flowed.

At first, I blamed myself. "What have I done to deserve this?" I cried out. Then, my emotions raged against God. "Lord, You can do anything. Why did You let this happen to Dennis?" But after my initial emotions flowed out, a sense of acceptance took hold. God has a plan for us all, I believed. He was allowing this to happen for a reason. I knew it. I believed it with all my heart. "Lord, if it is Your will, please save my son," I prayed.

My tears now dried, I returned to Dennis' room. Again, I sat by his side, talking to him and praying. The next day, relatives took over at home so Maureen could join me at the bedside of our beloved son. I met Maureen in the hospital lobby with a nurse who explained that Dennis' condition was serious, but the ultimate outcome was unknown. I held Maureen's hand tightly as we walked to Dennis' room. No words were necessary or adequate; only we truly understood the love we had for our son. Our pain was indescribable. The only comfort was in knowing we shared it with each other.

From the moment Dennis was born twenty years earlier, the world was a brighter place for me. "It's a boy!" the doctor had announced. Never had I experienced such happiness. Looking into his perfect little face, loved rushed through me to an extent I never imagined possible. As a policeman, I was a tough guy. But holding the miracle of my newborn son, I went soft inside. Life would never be the same.

Although Dennis had been given my name, as he grew I could see that he was not so much of a "chip off the old block." He was different. He let it all out and he took it all in. He loved everyone and was not afraid to show it. In turn, it seemed everyone loved him.

One of his earliest loves was baseball. He was smitten with it during his first Little League season. Dennis was an all-around athlete, but baseball was his true love. It was a joy to watch him field and hit with all the gusto only a baseball-loving boy can muster. One of my proudest moments was watching Dennis at fifteen smack a major-league home run. I'd often make deals with guys at work so I would not miss his games: "You cover me this afternoon and I'll cover you tomorrow morning."

At school, kids gravitated toward Dennis. A natural leader, he was elected vice president of his high school class. Besides sports, he was an altar boy who served with enthusiasm, and a loving son and a big brother always looked out for his younger siblings.

Seeing Dennis lying so still in a hospital bed was a sight I had difficulty accepting. Maureen never left his side except to sleep and eat. I could only bear short visits—coming and going throughout the day. His helplessness made be feel useless. I was his father. I had always been there for him before. But now, there was nothing I could do. It was a suffocating, crushing feeling.

After ten days, we knew one of us should return home. Our other children needed us, too. It made the most sense for me to get back to work and put a routine back into our home. "Good-bye, Dennis," I said, looking into my son's face. "I love you." My heart ached. Would I ever see him again? Would it ever be the way it was?

The prayers never stopped. And yet, I knew that God had a plan and I could only wait and accept that plan. Not quite two weeks after I returned home, the phone rang at 4 a.m. Before I even picked up the receiver, I knew my son had died. A piece of me died with him.

Maureen and I planned our son's funeral. We knew Dennis was loved by many, but we had no idea just how many. Lines weaved outside the funeral parlor. The funeral Mass was standing room only. Weeks later we still received letters from teachers, students, parents, and friends who shared their love of him with us. Dennis had touched so many people.

But as life once again became routine, I struggled to go on. My oldest son was gone. I would never again feel his arms around me or have his smiling face light up my life. The hole he left in my life was huge and black.

"God," I prayed. "I know Dennis is with You, but can You send me a sign to let me know he's all right?" I was searching for comfort, some sort of connection with my son.

Shortly after I had asked God for a sign, Maureen and I were having dinner at a restaurant when our cell phone rang. It was our daughter, Danielle.

The father of one of Dennis's friends had called to let us know that he discovered a new billboard hanging over Fenway Park. In the photo, his son, Joseph "Fitzy" Fitzpatrick, is clenching the home run ball he caught. His buddy, our son, Dennis, is sitting next to him, smiling wide under his Red Sox cap.

My sign. It was getting late, so the first thing in the morning Maureen and I headed to Fenway Park. Seeing our son's happy face over the stadium, tears of both joy and grief poured down our cheeks. That was our boy—our baseball-loving boy—smiling down at us. Our tears turned to laughter. Leave it to Dennis to pull off something like this.

Dennis had loved baseball. He was in his element, at a baseball game surrounded by friends. The picture was taken by the Red Sox photographer two years before he died. Of all the thousands of pictures, it was the one with my son that had been chosen. From that day forth, I began to breath easier and I experienced peace. I am OK now and I know my son is, too.

—Dennis Thomson

Dennis Thomson is a retired, 39-year veteran of the Boston Police Department. He and Maureen started a scholarship fund in memory of their son, Dennis, which is awarded to "all-around nice kids," not necessarily top students. Donations can be sent to the Dennis Thomson Scholarship Fund, 68 Freeman St., Quncy, MA 02170.

Faith Enough for Two

First grade taught me many different things. Dick jumped, Jane skipped, and both of them saw Spot run. I also couldn't help but notice that most of the other children had lunch pails with thermoses to match. Most girls my age had a different dress for each day of the week. Not only was I short on clothes, I had to take my bologna sandwich in a brown paper bag with no thermos. Drinking water from the school cooler was perfectly suited to our family budget.

By second grade, a flyer was passed around for joining Brownies. In a small town in Oklahoma, Brownies is the quintessential little girl experience. Needless to say, I was devastated when my mother had to explain that I couldn't be a Brownie because we could not afford the uniform and dues. My hopes for belonging, blending in, and being accepted were dashed.

The hurt in my father's eyes told me it pained him to deny his little girl this opportunity. My father told me that living in a dream world would only lead to pain and disappointment. He said that I needed to understand three very simple things: money marries money, good things happen to those who can afford them, and that it would take a miracle for me to be a Brownie. Then, he added, "Miracles do not exist."

It may seem that my father was cold, but he wasn't. His life had been a hard one. It was out of love that he handed down his life lessons. In his mind, it was a dose of reality and the sooner I accepted it, the less I would get hurt in the long run. This lack of faith in miracles did not meake sense to me.

I remember lying in bed that night with the Brownie flyer under my pillow, praying that my dad wasn't right. I wanted to believe that even if you didn't have money, you could still be worth something and your dreams could still come true. I loved my father, but he seemed to not have all of the information. Miracles had been scarce for him. I wondered if it was because he didn't know how to believe in them. I was convinced the secret was in the believing and I was determined to believe enough for both of us.

The next day at school, my second-grade teacher, Mrs. Stone, gave us an assignment. She had us write a paper on our favorite color. My friends picked from every color of the rainbow, while I picked brown. I wrote that brown was the color of the dirt and good things grow in dirt, and that brown was the color of the bark on the truck of a tree and it was the trunk that held up the branches that held the fruit. And finally, I wrote that brown was the color of a uniform of the most wonderful organization in the world, Brownies. But sadly, I wrote, I wasn't going to get to be one because we had no money for the uniform or the dues.

Almost two weeks later, Mrs. Stone asked if I could stay after school for a few minutes. Following the school bell, she took me into her office and told me that she had a surprise for me. Opening a box, my eyes just about popped out of my head. A Brownie uniform! She kept apologizing that it wasn't new. It was her niece's old uniform. She asked if I could try it on. My torn and shabby slip made me hesitate, but I could live through the embarrassment if the uniform would just fit. It did.

It was wonderful. Mrs. Stone even had the little beanie hat that went with it. I knew God had answered my prayers. I knew Mrs. Stone was the kindest woman in the world. And I knew from that moment on that my father was wrong; not because he was bad, but because someone must have lied to him about miracles. When I put on my uniform, I knew I wasn't meant to be just poor white trash. I was meant to be something wonderful; I was meant to be a Brownie.

The big annual event in Brownies was the father-daughter dinner. I had never had an evening out alone with my dad. My mom had him borrow a suit from one of our neighbors. That night, I thought that my dad was the most handsome man there. The Brownies had prepared a song for the daughters to sing to their dads. Just before we began to sing, my father lifted me up and stood me next to him on a chair. As I began to sing the song we had learned entitled "Let Me Call You Sweetheart," my father began to sing with me in harmony. It was a glorious sound.

There were tears in both our eyes as we finished singing. Then he leaned over and whispered into my ear, "When I look at you, my little Brownie, and see you in that uniform, I can believe in miracles." My heart soared. I *had* believed enough for both of us.

For a moment, nothing else mattered. We were a father and a daughter experiencing one of the richest moments of my life. In that moment miracles were as real as we were, and the hope created for me out of that experience has led me forth ever since.

—Dawn Billings

Dawn Billings is the president of The Joy of Connecting™ an Atlanta-based, innovative marketing company. She has been a licensed professional counselor for more than twenty years. Dawn is the author of more than fifteen books. To contact Dawn to speak or order books, call 1-877-411-6611 or 918-605-1492. You can learn more at www.DawnBillings.com or e-mail her at ChooseToBeGreat@aol.com

My Dad is Still With Me

Like so many fathers and sons, my dad and I seemed to always talk past one another. I loved him, but it seemed we were incapable of communicating—especially when it came to sharing our emotions for each other. And religion ... that was not even on the radar screen for us.

When a young man leaves home for college, he often forgets about church in the midst of his newfound freedom. Ironically, it was my father who quit going to church, while I recommitted myself to Christ. My dad was very intelligent and a voracious reader, but the spiritual seemed to hold no appeal for him.

Then, he developed the emphysema that would eventually take him. As the disease progressed, his lungs began to labor with each breath. Dad's world became the confines of the bedroom, bathroom. and kitchen table—the only places his portable oxygen tank allowed him to reach. Luckily, the oxygen tube reached long enough to allow its prisoner access to the computer. It was there, through emails, that I began to connect with Dad on a deeper level than ever before.

One day, realizing my dad would likely not be long for this world, I felt compelled to bring up the topic of faith one more time. I had done so other times over the years but without success. I asked him why he seemed not to want God in his life.

"Son," he responded, "I do love God. I just don't know if He loves me. I have started praying the Lord's Prayer whenever my breathing gets particularly bad. It helps calm me down. But I really don't know how to pray. In fact, with all I've done in my life, I really don't know if God wants to hear from me anymore."

Reading his words filled my head with Scripture verses I could use to show Dad that God still loved him. Interruptions prevented me from responding that day, but by morning, I turned on my computer, ready to encourage my father in his faith.

As my email box came into focus, I discovered Dad had already written to me again. "Dear Marc, You won't believe what happened to me. I know it was God speaking to me. After I emailed you yesterday, I went to bed to read. I picked up the Grishom book I was reading called *The Mission* and started where I had left off. In the story, immediately the main character asked the missionary, "I really don't know how to pray. How should I do it?" and then the missionary taught him. Marc, these were the very words I wrote you yesterday. I know somehow it was God telling me He loved me."

It was then that I trusted that my father knew Jesus. He did not just say, "Wow! What a coincidence." His heart had become, by grace, open to the inspiration of God. He knew and he believed.

Dad died in February of 2002. A priest came to him the afternoon of his death and prayed with him. It would surely appear that he died at peace with God, but after our lifetime of miscommunication, there was still a part of me wondering if he had been ready to meet Jesus at the end. I thought of him often and missed him terribly. I wished I knew if he was really OK—if he was with Our Lord.

On my dad's birthday, I went to visit my mother to make sure she was doing OK without him. When I returned home, there was a small wrapped package on my desk. I opened it and found a delightful, hand-carved statue. A man who had seen me on EWTN television hosting the March for Life in Washington, D.C., had carved the statue of me with my funny hat on and holding a microphone. Unbeknownst to this stranger, my father's main hobby had been woodcarving. He carved small figures exactly like the one this man had just made me.

On the shelf right in front of me, where I could always see it, was just such a carving. My father had done this carving of an old man that looked just like him in the last days of his life. I set the two figures together and I knew. I knew that this was a message from Dad, coming through the veil. I knew that with God's merciful permission, he was letting me know that he was fine; that he was with Jesus.

I thank God for the little things. I believe that life's little coincidences are God's way of showing His love and care for us. And it is in the little things that I still feel close to my father and trust that he will always be with me.

—Marcus Grodi

Marcus Grodi served nine years as a Protestant minister before he and his family were received into the Catholic Church in 1992. He is the president of the Coming Home Network International, a non-profit Catholic lay apostolate that helps non-Catholic clergy and laity come home to the Catholic Church. The author of the novel How Firm a Foundation *and the editor/author of* Journeys Home, *Marcus hosts a weekly television program on EWTN called* The Journey Home *and a weekly live radio program called* Deep In Scripture.

Children Lost and Found

All children are miracles—gifts of our loving and generous God. This we know. Some, however, are more miraculous than others due to the circumstances of their conception or birth. This is the story of two of our "miracle children."

Soon after we exchanged vows at California's Mission San Antonio de Padua, Christina and I found we had begun our marriage and our family almost simultaneously. Barely nine months after our June 1984 wedding, Christina gave birth to our firstborn, Michael, in mid-April. Four months later, we learned Christina was pregnant with our second child, due the following April, just one year after the first.

We were absolutely open to God's will and providence in determining our family size, so we were grateful and humbled to be so blessed by Him. Nevertheless, it was a difficult development, particularly for Christina. Life was moving along a bit too rapidly. While we were yet adjusting to parenthood and even to married life itself, our family had already doubled in size.

Little were we aware that a remarkable turn of events that year would draw us ever closer to Him—and to each other.

Christina and I had spent a Saturday afternoon with little Michael in downtown Oakland, not far from the apartment where we lived at the time, treating ourselves to lunch and exploring some of the local department stores. Later that afternoon, as we attended Mass at St. Francis Cathedral, Christina suddenly began first to feel sick, then crampy. My concern grew in proportion to her pain.

After Mass, we arrived home to find that Christina had been bleeding. Fearing an imminent miscarriage, we phoned Christina's nurse-midwife, who directed us to the emergency room at Alta Bates Hospital in nearby Berkeley. Our hearts raced anxiously as we prayed in the car, first to the babysitter's house and then to the hospital. Christina, perhaps feeling a bit of guilt for her reservations about having another child already, wept silently as she mourned her anticipated loss. For my part, I held out a margin of hope for a lesser, treatable alternative explanation of the troubling symptom.

As we waited in the trauma room for the doctor to arrive, Christina and I decided it would be prudent to baptize the unborn child. Unclear of the validity of our actions but certain of God's mercy, I dribbled a handful of tap water over my wife's abdomen, pronouncing the words of baptism as I did. That rite, however clumsy, ushered in an interesting transformation: The sacrament seemed to give Christina a new hope for the baby's survival, while I suddenly felt a spirit of peace and acceptance that the child would be entering the waiting arms of God.

The doctor arrived and quickly came to her diagnosis of an "inevitable miscarriage." She recommended that Christina be admitted for a D&C to ensure that the miscarriage would be completed without risk of infection.

The term "D&C"—dilation and curettage—struck a chord with us because it is the same procedure used in many abortions. In the case of clear miscarriage, the procedure would be morally permissible. But we had some questions for the kind physician: Could she guarantee that our unborn child was already dead? She admitted she could not be 100 percent positive, although she was nearly certain of it. Was

Christina in any kind of immediate danger? No, she was not. The surgical procedure was strictly preventative.

Under those conditions, we answered, given our Catholic moral principles, we could not consent to the D&C. Could we instead go home, complete the miscarriage there, and watch for signs of fever or infection that might require medical intervention? The doctor said she wouldn't recommend it, but we were within our rights to take that course of action. So we did.

The miscarriage progressed for a few days without incident, and together we mourned the child we never knew. We accepted God's will, but little understood it. A dark cloud of mild depression enveloped my mind and weighed on my heart, and my wife felt similarly. It was a very difficult time for both of us.

The nurse-midwife phoned that week with her sympathies and set an appointment with Christina for an exam to ensure there were no complications from the miscarriage. That Friday, we went to the appointment.

As the nurse-midwife began her examination, she noticed Christina's belly had not "gone down" at all since miscarriage. Puzzled and looking for clues, she applied the ultrasound monitor to Christina's abdomen. Her eyes quickly widened to saucer-like proportions. "Oh, my God!" she gasped. She had picked up, loud and strong, the unmistakable and familiar sound of a fetal heartbeat!

We all were flabbergasted. How could this be? Had our little number-two child, against all odds, survived the turmoil of an "inevitable miscarriage"? The joy I felt in that moment defies expression. It was a glimmer perhaps of what the Apostles felt when they realized their Lord had been raised from the dead. Somehow, by the grace of God, our child had been spared. Unworthily, we had received a miracle among miracles.

To help solve the mystery, our nurse-midwife ordered that sonogram images be taken at Alta Bates immediately. The images and the radiologist's evaluation soon revealed what had happened. There, positioned high in my wife's womb, was an intact amniotic sac with a living child within; and there, down low, was what appeared to be an empty sac where a child once had been.

What had happened? Unbeknownst to any of us, Christina had been carrying twins—fraternal twins, each with his or her own sac and placenta. For whatever reason, possibly an early fetal death, one miscarried. The other was saved, oblivious to the drama that had unfolded in her watery neighborhood.

How affirming not only of the value of human life, but also about the wisdom of our Catholic moral teaching! For if we had been any less meticulous about the bioethical questions of our situation, we might have consented to the D&C. We would have lost both children, never knowing of the second child's existence. I thank God, with a shudder, that we made such prudent choices that day.

Although the disbelief of some members of our extended family caused Christina and me no small pain, in the aftermath we found our marriage was doubly blessed. The deeply spiritual experience helped to draw us closer together as a couple, dashing many of the issues that had made our first year together more challenging and uniting us more intimately with God and each other. From that day, Christina's pregnancy proceeded normally, culminating in the birth of our first daughter, Monica Mary, in April 1986.

In an ironic twist, Monica today is a junior biology major at the University of Notre Dame, and she has a special career interest in the field of bioethics.

∽

Fast forward a dozen years. Since Monica's miracle, God had blessed us with more children—and frequently so. The births of Catherine, Raymond, Sophia, Adrienne, and Mark had swelled our ranks to nine, the last four born during our nearly ten years living in Montana. After six successful midwife-assisted home births, Mark was the first to be born in a hospital.

We were expecting child number eight when I accepted a new professional opportunity in another state. So in June 1998, with Christina about eleven weeks pregnant, I moved my family to our new home in northeast Indiana.

Another miracle would be waiting for us there.

On August 18, nine weeks after our arrival and twenty weeks into the pregnancy, we celebrated Christina's birthday at home. As we cleared the table, the children were all excited. The cake was decorated, ice cream was thawing on the counter, and gifts were waiting to be opened.

Just as were about to sit down for dessert, however, Christina called me aside with some startling news: Her water had broken. We knew this meant a hospital visit and possibly another miscarriage. Not wanting to spoil the evening for the children, however, we put on a brave face and went through with the birthday celebration. It was not easy to keep smiling, but we covered well the real anxiety and pain we felt inside.

When all was done and the children were tucked into bed, we told the oldest two kids about our plans to seek medical care. By phone, Christina's ob-gyn recommended she go not to one of the larger and fancier health-care facilities in the area, but to St. Joseph Hospital, an older, inner-city facility. Once checked in there, Christina was assigned to a room in the maternity ward and we learned it was very likely we were about to lose our baby.

At twenty weeks, a child is not viable outside the womb. Every doctor the ob-gyn consulted advised her to let nature take its course. Our doctor, knowing we were devout Catholics, ordered bed rest and convalescence in the hope of forestalling labor until viability was reached at least. St. Joseph, she intimated, was perhaps the only area hospital that would accommodate a bed request for such a purpose.

I stayed with Christina late into the night and we discussed our uncertain prospects. We had no idea how long this drama would take to unfold, but we were prepared to do whatever it took to save our baby. Christina would stay in the hospital; I had to manage a household while keeping my day job. Complicating matters further, August 19 was the children's first day at their new school. I went home for a scant few hours' sleep.

Early the next morning, I phoned a neighbor whom I had barely met, and she consented to watch Adrienne and Mark that day. I hauled the older kids to their parish school and went on to the hospital.

A neonatologist from neighboring Lutheran Hospital (which had ties to St. Joseph) began to monitor the case and was encouraging to Christina. If she could get to twenty-three weeks, he told her, he could do a lot to save the baby. Twenty-three weeks thus became our goal, a benchmark that gave us some hope. Christina took on that cross heroically.

Support from utter strangers was immediate and overwhelming. Promises of prayers came flooding in from all directions. Our parish school, St. Jude, began collecting donations of groceries and sending them home with our kids each day. At my workplace, Our Sunday Visitor Inc., I was little more than a name on a phone directory to most employees, and yet volunteers provided hot meals, casseroles, or pizza gift certificates on an almost daily basis. Although I tried to keep the household running as "normally" as possible, the influx of groceries, meals, and prayers proved an invaluable assist.

With a rotation of babysitters and carpools arranged, I returned to work quickly. Sleep and leisure were luxuries. I'd visit my wife most mornings before work, and I'd take the children to see their mom in the evenings. Dinner, housekeeping, homework help and school-lunch preparation melded into a continuum of activity. I suppose it was a trial for me, but I never lost sight of the fact that my wife and unborn child were struggling with much bigger issues than I was.

Some nights I'd return to the hospital alone, bringing my wife a milkshake or some other treat foreign to a hospital meal plan. We had to maintain our close bond despite the separation. As the days wore into weeks, family stress became more evident, surfacing particularly among the children. Some did not understand why Mommy could not come home; those who did understand grew frustrated with the situation.

When Christina reached twenty-three weeks, we celebrated the milestone. Our doctors began to discuss whether it was best to remove the child from her compromised, nearly waterless womb by Caesarean section or to allow the child to develop there as long as possible. The latter view prevailing for now, our neonatologist injected

Christina with a steroid to help the baby's lungs in the event of premature birth. The wait continued.

On the night of September 18, one month after Christina was admitted to the hospital and nearly twenty-five weeks into her pregnancy, I found myself exhausted from work and stress. I worried that Christina might remain hospitalized until the baby's January 1 due date. I also feared that the child might die despite all our efforts, and that Christina's own life could be endangered. I was spent, and had only God's providence on which to rely. He never tests us beyond what we can bear, and in times like these I thank God that I'm such a weak man.

As I prayed before falling asleep that night, I tried to block out all my pain, stress, and fatigue as I meditated on the Jesus Prayer: "Jesus Christ, son of God, be merciful to me, a sinner." As I did, I felt myself being lifted out of my sorry state. For a few brief moments—maybe fifteen seconds, maybe fifteen minutes—I felt totally at peace, pain-free, stress-free, fatigue-free. It was a small gift of God's presence, and I was grateful the respite it provided. I dozed off to a rare, deep slumber.

A few hours later, I was awakened with a start by the insistent ring of the telephone at my bedside. After first answering my alarm clock, I found the handset and asked wearily, "Hello?" It was Christina, and it was about 1:18 a.m. "Honey, I just had the baby," she told me. "She's alive, she's breathing, and she's beautiful! Come quickly."

I said "OK" and hung up the phone. As I sat up numbly in bed, I wondered whether that phone conversation had actually happened. Was it a dream? I had to presume not. Pulling on some clothes, I woke Michael with the news and drove to St. Joseph Hospital, still debating whether the call was real or imagined.

When I arrived at the maternity ward, the neonatologist, ob/gyn, and several staffers were on the scene. There in a portable incubator was a tiny baby, a little girl, wrapped in a blanket and connected to an array of breathing tubes and various monitors. She was doing fine so far. Born at just under twenty-five weeks, our little girl weighed in at one pound, ten ounces. And she was alive.

My wife was radiant as she told her story. The birth had occurred suddenly and unexpectedly, and she had caught the baby herself before she could even call for a nurse. The duty nurse did not normally work maternity and was moderately flustered when she first saw the very premature infant. I chuckled at the irony: After weeks of hospitalization and medical attention, my wife essentially had an unassisted birth.

I had long wanted to name a child Jane Frances, after St. Jane Frances de Chantal. When I pointed out to Christina that the whole crisis began on St. Jane's feast day, she quickly agreed to my suggestion.

Christina would stay another night at St. Joseph, but I headed to Lutheran Hospital where Jane Frances would be cared for in the neonatal intensive care unit (NICU). I watched as expert nurses set up her warming isolette and explained the various meters, ventilators, and gadgets. Jane Frances would sleep on a receiving blanket in a plastic box covered with Saran wrap and warmed by heat lamps, an environment that simulates the womb as much as possible. A "minimum stimulation" protocol would help her conserve valuable calories.

I broke the good news to my children at breakfast the following morning. They were excited—not only about the baby, but also because they knew their mom would soon be home at last.

Christina was discharged the following day, and together we visited little Jane. Because the NICU environment must be kept so sterile, visitors must scrub with anti-bacterial soap and wear surgical gowns and masks. Because we could not touch the child, we were mere spectators. I recall how we looked at our daughter and at each other with drained and exhausted eyes, knowing that Jane's life was in the hands of the attending doctors and nurses—and of God.

The following evening, we entered the NICU with Jane's godmother, a proxy, and our associate pastor to celebrate the Sacrament of Baptism. There, as we stood about the isolette wearing yellow surgical garb, Father led a most moving baptismal rite. We had no candle, but a plethora of hospital-issue white garments; we made the Sign of the Cross in the air over the child in our latex-gloved hands. Holding a plastic syringe in his hand as he pronounced the words of baptism, Father squeezed three tiny droplets of sterilized water onto Jane's forehead, effectively administering the sanctifying grace promised by Christ.

As the rite ended, we asked Father if he thought it might be a good idea to give Jane the sacrament of anointing as well, something the Church gives to seriously ill individuals. He smiled broadly. "Let's just wait and see what baptism can do," he said with an infectious confidence.

In those first days in the NICU, doctors and nurses gave consistently positive reports on Jane's progress. But they also were emphatic about the risks of complications that could happen at any time, particularly for one born so early and so small. Cerebral palsy, retardation, blindness, crippling illnesses, lung and heart damage, or compromised immune systems remained threats to our precious child. We couldn't help but notice how other babies in the NICU seemed to be suffering so many worse problems than Jane, and it made us almost hesitant to discuss our baby's health with other NICU parents whose child might be having a much tougher battle for life and health.

I understood why the NICU staff did not want to raise our expectations to excess, but nothing could shake me from believing that Jane would survive without chronic medical issues. The words of our associate pastor, holy man that he was, kept resounding within my ears: "Let's wait and see what baptism can do." I believed him. Besides, we had seen a special miracle in our lives already with Monica's birth, and with so many friends and strangers praying for our baby, we were very confident that Jane Frances would thrive.

And thrive she did. Soon, she was off the infant ventilator, and Christina was able to hold her outside the isolette and even breastfeed her. By about mid-November, we were able to bring most of our other children to the NICU to meet their new sister. It was a brief but wonderful bonding experience for them all.

On Thanksgiving Day, we had a very emotional visit to the NICU. Jane was doing very well, but she was not yet ready to come home to us. I teared up at the thought of gathering for Thanksgiving dinner with the newest member of our family missing. We turned our hopes and prayers toward bringing her home by Christmas.

Mid-December arrived, and we still weren't sure when Jane would be discharged to our care. We did not want to go through another holiday without her; our children would ask us frequently whether their baby sister would be with us soon. Her crib was ready, and our hearts were more than ready, but Jane herself was not.

On December 17, our neonatologist surprised us with the news: Jane could go home tomorrow! She had reached five-and-a-half pounds, was eating and functioning extremely well, and now her medical care could be accomplished as an outpatient. So one week before Christmas, our entire family was together at last. We had received our greatest, most longed-for Christmas gift ever.

The Jane miracle went on and on. There was the pediatric ophthalmologist who diagnosed her in early 1999 with advanced retinopathy of prematurity, an irreversible complication that frequently causes blindness; a week later, after many prayers and novenas on Jane's behalf, the same doctor reversed that diagnosis when his follow-up examination revealed no evidence of retinopathy whatsoever. There were Jane's two hospital stays in her second year of life, when each time she emerged unscathed after spending several days in an oxygen tent with a spasmodic cough and pneumonia caused by respiratory syncytial virus.

Today, Jane Frances is an impish, intelligent, and articulate second-grader, precocious enough to tell total strangers the story of how she's a "miracle child." She is indeed.

Every child is a miracle, some more miraculous than others. Our family experiences of pregnancy and childbirth, of lost twins and surviving preemies, only serve to confirm and strengthen what we have always believed: We must trust in God's providence, trust in the wisdom of the Church, and trust ever so strongly in the amazing power of prayer.

We've seen it all work miracles.

—Gerald Korson

Gerald Korson is the editor and manager of Our Sunday Visitor, *the largest-circulating national Catholic newspaper in the United States. He and his wife, Christina, reside in Fort Wayne, Ind., with their ten children, including Jane's two little sisters, Amy and Susanna.*

Miracle Delivery

"Stand still, Mary," my mother scolded. "Or I can't get these dress measurements right." I was a typical nine-year-old girl, full of energy and mostly oblivious to the poverty that nipped at my parents' heels. It was 1939 and the Depression was in full force. Once my father was out of work, poverty no longer "nipped" at us; it had us in its jaws. My dad was a hard worker and a loving father and husband. The pain of not being able to provide for his family must certainly have run deep. There were eight of us children and a ninth baby was on the way.

Without employment, my family had no choice but to take advantage of President Roosevelt's Federal Relief Program. We qualified to receive coal to heat our rented farm house. During the warmer months, our large garden, a blackberry patch, a cow and chickens kept or tummies full and even allowed us to make money on the extras. But now, with winter upon us, our own canned goods and some government surplus and clothing were all we had to help us through. I watched my mother filling out paperwork and writing down my measurements, but my youthful mind did not fully comprehend my parents' worries until one evening.

During supper, our parents revealed to us that our situation had become dire. Unless we received a relief order of coal that night, all eight of us would need to go to the Children's Home the next day. I looked anxiously around the table at my siblings and parents. Fear was etched on their faces. I could not imagine being taken away from my loving

parents. Yet, they could not let us all freeze to death. There
was nowhere else to turn, but we knew we always had God.
After our simple meal, we all got on our knees to finish
the ninth and last day of our novena to St. Joseph and to
pray the rosary. Our prayers were heartfelt and desperate.
We trusted that God could find a way to help us. Just as we
were ending the rosary, the sound of a truck engine could be
heard coming up our lane. *Could it be the relief order of coal
our father had requested?* we all wondered.

My father jumped up and grabbed his coat, saying, "I'll
help him unload it." We finished our rosary in great joy!

"Thank God," my mother sighed, clasping her rosary.

"Now we don't have to go to the Children's Home!" one
of my siblings shouted.

But when my father came back into the house, his face
bore a puzzled expression.

"I don't think that was the relief order," he told our
mother. "I never saw that man before, and he didn't give me
a paper to sign." As we prepared for bed in a house that was
a little warmer, we all wondered who the delivery man had
been. The next day another load of coal arrived. My mother
told the driver, who was her cousin, "We got a load of coal
last night from another driver."

Her cousin chuckled and said, "I'm the only one around
here who delivers relief orders for coal. If you got a load of
coal last night, St. Joseph must have brought it!"

Whether it was St. Joseph or an angel, we don't know.
We never received a bill for the coal. Our Blessed Mother
didn't want her children to have to go away to the Children's
Home. She had taken our prayers to her Son and God had
answered them.

There were not many Christmas presents under the
tree that year, but Daddy managed to get enough wood to

make us a wooden sled on runners. Many happy hours were spent riding that sled down the sloping grounds around our farm.

My father eventually got hired for the Works Project Administration also begun by President Roosevelt. Things got better financially for us, but for me, the best part of my childhood was the love and faith my parents gave us.

—Mary F. Pitstick

Mary Pitstick grew up in a devout Catholic family, the sixth of ten children. She and her husband, Paul, reside on a farm near Fairborn, Ohio. They have seven grown children, nineteen grandchildren, and five great-grandchildren.

An Adopting Father

I mounted the stairs that led to the kitchen, home from a full day of work at the EWTN studios in Irondale, Alabama. I had recently started hosting my live television show for young adults, *Life on the Rock*, and I had relocated with my wife and daughter from Ohio to Alabama to a modest home with an extra bedroom.

My wife, Emily, was busy in the kitchen when I rounded the corner to greet her. To my surprise, she stood by the stove with one of our pet cats in a sling around her shoulders. "Oh, isn't that cute," I smiled rubbing Nic the cat's whiskers and kissing Emily.

"He wants me to hold him all the time, so I put him in this," Emily grinned a bit sheepishly.

I set my brief case on the floor and cocked my head as I looked at the two of them. "You know what?" I declared as a brilliant idea struck me. Though I wasn't too fond of cats, Emily liked cats a lot. Seeing how much she liked to baby the cat, I said, "What you need is another cat!" We already had two Tonkinese breed cats. I thought Emily would be thrilled with my offer. I was not prepared for her comeback.

Her expression turned to a scowl as she snapped, "I don't want to raise cats! I want to raise baby humans!"

Whew! Where did that come from? I wondered, feeling it was time for me to exit. *I thought we laid that idea to rest.* I tried to sound reasonable. "We tried all sorts of ways to have more children but with no success. I thought we had come to terms with not having any more. We have a wonderful daughter already!" Several years ago I had laid the sadness of trying unsuccessfully to have more children at the feet of Jesus and had accepted the disappointment. I had gone on with my life and career, and I was just beginning to see the days when our eleven-year-old would be grown up and Emily and I would travel together while I spoke at conferences around the country. She could be a speaker also and we'd see the world together. I didn't particularly like traveling alone and sleeping in hotels without Emily, so this new chapter down the road looked like a sunny one.

The look in Emily's eyes as she glared at me told me that the issue was not at rest with her. "Now we have a house with an extra room and are making a stable living. Why can't we adopt a child?" she asked, untying the cat and scooting him out of the kitchen.

"We've tried adopting!" I exclaimed. I thought to myself, *Didn't she remember the many avenues we had pursued in the past with that?* I could not understand her. "We already have a terrific child!" I said.

"As Catholics, we understand the importance of children and being open to life. I can't stop thinking about what we could offer another child," she explained. Emily had just come into the Church a little over a year earlier, following my lead and decision to return to the Church after several years away.

I agreed totally with openness to life, but I hadn't been thinking along the lines of adoption recently until she brought up the idea. I had come to a comfortable resolve with the idea of only one child after our years of struggling with infertility. I left the kitchen to go change my clothes. For the moment we let the topic hang in the air.

While I kept busy at work, Emily kept busy checking our options. She called about foster parenting. She checked with Catholic social services about adopting and began inquiring about how to get an adoption home study done.

She talked to other acquaintances and neighbors who had adopted their children. The idea of adopting became more real to me as she continued with the search.

One day after she told me of the latest updates, I tried to put some reality into it. We had been disappointed several other times we had attempted to adopt years earlier, and I didn't want Emily to get her hopes up too high.

At last she said with a few tears, "I just want to love!"

I could feel her deep desire, so I decided it was time for me to pitch in with this endeavor. "OK!" I responded. "We'll tell everyone we know that we're looking to adopt and see what happens." Now Emily was smiling like a kid in a candy store and I felt strangely uplifted by the idea myself.

Knowing from past experience how difficult it is to find babies in this country and how expensive it is to find children overseas, I was not prepared just a few short weeks later to get a call from one of Emily's acquaintances. "I know a college student who is looking for a Catholic family to adopt her baby. She has one family lined up, but it doesn't seem to be working out. Would you be interested?"

Emily was beside herself with excitement. "The baby is due in six weeks! What do you think?"

I couldn't think. It certainly seemed to be God's great timing and maybe his sense of humor, too. I was totally unprepared. *Was it possible to love an adopted child the way I loved our daughter, Carly?* I wondered. *Was it possible to love a second child? Could we afford it? Could I take on that responsibility?* The more excited Emily became, the more my head spun.

Our friend set up a phone interview with the young woman. Emily sat on our bed waiting for the phone to ring as I paced and worried. She called and asked us many questions on how we would raise her: Would she learn music? Do we have pets? After her call I felt compassion for the sweet woman who found herself in such a difficult place. I felt even more convinced that God was orchestrating this for us and for the birthmother. We ended the conversation without a conclusion and agreed to speak again after we looked over the finances. We would need to cover the doctor and hospital bills..

I had no idea where I could scrape up so much money in such a short time. We had nothing in the bank. When I had resigned as a Protestant pastor two years before to return to the Catholic Church, I had lost my source of income. Over the previous year, we had depleted all our reserves except for a bit we had used as a down payment on our house. These new bills seemed very large. I couldn't see how it could possibly work so quickly. Bills for the home study, the lawyer, and so many other things involved in adopting loomed in my thoughts.

A few hours before the scheduled call with the birthmother to give her our answer, I voiced my fear to Emily that maybe we couldn't go through with it. Emily sat sobbing on the bed. "That's all I want to do!" she cried. "I want to raise children. I just want to love!"

My heart burned inside and God's peace suddenly filled me. "Emily, we'll make it work somehow. I don't know how, but I know this is important. We should do it. We'll believe God that he will help us." I just couldn't say no to Emily when I realized how badly she wanted more children. I, too, felt that this baby was ours and had come to want it as badly. It was the desire of our hearts. We had to trust God to get us through.

The next few weeks were a whirlwind with home study questionnaires and interviews, trips to the lawyer, plans for the birthmother to fly to Alabama to stay with our friend.

Part of our bedroom was changed into a nursery with Carly's old crib and changing table. The cats found the crib to be a wonderful napping spot. *You boys are in for the surprise of your life!* I told them as the thought echoed in my mind, "So are you, Jeff. That baby is on its way!"

A week before the baby was due, her birth mother arrived. We were delighted to meet her and found it both a strange and close experience at the same time. When the baby's due date came, the birth mother was induced and by five o'clock, our little Jacqueline Joy was born. I had to be back to the EWTN studio for my live show where I announced Jaki's birth like any proud father. I rushed over to the hospital directly after the show to see my little girl for the first time. Emily was allowed to stay in one of the hospital rooms with Jaki until Jaki was ready to be released. Emily and Carly were fussing over the little bundle as I hurried into the room. They placed her into my arms; instantly I felt a bond to her and tears welled up in eyes.

"I would die to for you, Jaki," I said swept with emotion. This helpless infant captured me entirely and I knew beyond knowing that I loved her as I loved my first daughter. My love was no different. I think all of our cheeks were sore from all the smiling we did when we looked at our newest family member.

Just as wonderfully, twenty-one months later we adopted Antonia Teresa as a newborn. She, too, filled me with the same love and emotion as for the other two daughters. In adopting these beautiful children, I have come to know something of God's love for me. Romans 8:15 tells us, "When we cry 'Abba! Father!' it is the Spirit himself bearing witness with our spirit that we are children of God." All of God's children are adopted. Adoption is not just a theological idea—it is a reality for everyone who goes by the name "Christian."

—Jeff Cavins

Jeff Cavins is the co-creator and one of the editors of the Amazing Grace *series. His biography appears at the end of the book.*

In God's Hands

I always envisioned getting married and having a family, but at thirty-seven years of age I was still single. That's when I met Patricia. I was in Central Park with a friend. Patricia was also there with a friend who knew my friend. We bumped into each other and made introductions. Patricia, a dark-eye beauty, immediately got my attention. We all went out to dinner together and Patricia and I, not wanting the night to end, stayed up talking past three in the morning.

She had stolen my heart, and two years later we married. For Patricia, marriage and a family had been her dream since she was a little girl. I was content to take life as God led me. Once He led me to Patricia, however, I agreed that we should start a family immediately. After all, I was thirty-nine by then. Patricia was twenty-seven, but she could not wait for us to have children.

After six months and still no children, Patricia decided it was time to see a doctor. Her doctor suggested that she relax and just give it a little more time. Then, one morning, I awoke to Patricia's cries for help. She was bleeding heavily. I rushed her to the doctor where an ultrasound revealed a fibroid tumor the size of an orange in her uterus.

Although the tumor was benign it put a constant pressure on and stabbing pain in Patricia's belly. It also made her periods longer and heavier. "What should I do?" she asked. The doctor advised doing nothing. "If we try to remove such a large fibroid, the scar tissue would make conception impossible," he said. "And you might bleed so much that we would have to end up performing a hysterectomy." The doctor felt that in spite of the tumor, Patricia might still achieve pregnancy.

It was unthinkable to Patricia that we would not have children. As the months passed and still no baby, I often found her in tears. "We'll find a way to have children," I would comfort her, but I knew my words were hollow. I could not promise her anything. Only God could do that.

"Lord, if it is Your will, please allow us to have children," I prayed. Patricia often took her lunch hour and spent it praying in church. When five more months passed without a child, Patricia decided to see a fertility specialist. "The fibroid is so large it's a hindrance to your conception," he said. "But even without it, your fallopian tubes are blocked so you could not get pregnant."

The doctor's only advice to us was that Patricia should have a hysterectomy. Patricia shook with grief. I put my arm around her and kissed her cheek, wet with tears. "Baby or no baby, I love you," I told her. I was disappointed, too, but having Patricia as my wife had already fulfilled by dreams. If we could not have children, at least we would have each other. I knew it was harder for Patricia to accept. My prayers continued for a child, but now I also asked God to help Patricia to accept whatever God's will was for us, even if it did not include children.

Then, one morning a friend called Patricia with some amazing news. She had just read about a doctor that used a new technique to remove fibroid tumors in a way that allowed women to still become pregnant. Patricia looked him up that morning and we had an appointment scheduled for two months later. After two-and-a-half years of bad news and disappointments, both of us braced ourselves for the possibility of more of the same.

I went with Patricia to see Dr. Ernst Bartsich in Manhattan. Dr. Bartsich announced that Patricia's tumor had grown to the size of a cantaloupe. "That is what is blocking your tubes, nothing else," he stated. Patricia and I looked at each other and then at the doctor. "Do you think that you can you help me? " she asked, cautiously.

"Yes," he replied confidently. Dr. Bartsich was making it his mission to avoid unnecessary hysterectomies by finding alternatives. "You seem like a perfect candidate for myomectomey, a procedure to remove fibroids while leaving the uterus intact, " he explained . By using ultrasound technology, there would not be any lasting scar tissue that would prevent conception "You will be pregnant within six months," he promised.

I looked at Patricia again. I felt the hope that I saw in her eyes. *Pregnant in six months?* I thought to myself. *Could it be?* After all our disappointment, I could not help but to hold back. Neither did I want Patricia to get her hopes up only to be crushed again. *Could this be the answer to our prayers?* I wondered. *We'll see.*

A month later, Patricia had the surgery. She was a week in the hospital and needed a full month of recovery. I worried that all this pain and suffering for Patricia might be in vain, yet I knew there was no choice for her. She had to try this. Now, the rest would be in God's hands.

Six months later, I received a call from Patricia while I was at work. "I'm pregnant!" she cried.

"We're going to have a baby!"

After three years of disappointments, it took a few minutes for the news to sink in. I was going to be a father! Tears of joy and gratitude filled my eyes. It was God's will that we experience the blessing of a child.

Our daughter Solange was born a month premature. The feeling of becoming a father for the first time at the age of forty-two was the end of one very long journey and the beginning of a new one. My world was different now— bigger, richer, deeper. It was not just my wife that shared my life, but my own flesh and blood.

The immensity of my responsibility as a father began to hit me right away. Solange's prematurity was causing some complications. She had hypoglycemia—low blood sugar— and needed to be placed in the intensive care unit. The joy we experienced by becoming parents was dimmed when Patricia returned home without our little daughter. Until Solange's blood sugar could be stabilized, she would need to stay in the hospital. Our home felt suddenly empty with just the two of us. We were not complete without her.

Then, after Patricia had been home for two days, on September 11, 2001, two planes hit and destroyed the World Trade Center towers. The city of New York and our country was in shock. For me, the crisis was personal. Roads were closed so I could not get to the hospital to bring my baby the breast milk that Patricia was pumping for her. My little girl needed this milk, but I could not get it to her. A sick feeling of helplessness and fear shot through me. *What kind of a world had my little girl been born into? How could I protect her and care for her?* I wondered.

It was twelve hours before I was able to get to the hospital with milk for our baby. When I got there, her room was empty. "Where is my baby?" I asked a nurse, shaking with panic. The babies' ICU had been moved to make room for possible victims from the World Trade Center. Solange had been moved to the other side of the floor. Relief and love poured through me when I reached my daughter's bassinet.

"Daddy's here," I said softly. "Everything is going to be all right."

And yet, my initiation into fatherhood had revealed so clearly to me that it was not within my power to make everything all right—not for my precious daughter and not for the world. We were in God's hands. He had answered our prayers and given us a daughter. There were no guarantees in life except that God was with us and would hear our prayers.

When Solange was a month old, we brought her home. She filled us with love and joy beyond measure. Then, by the next year, we welcomed another little miracle into the world: Isabelle. Today, at ages four and three, our two little girls are the apple of my eye. Fatherhood for me is more rewarding than I ever imagined. We bought a house on Long Island and Patricia stays home to care for our family.

I am truly a blessed man with a wonderful wife and two beautiful girls. We have God to thank for everything and we never forget that . We begin and end each day in prayer and we never stop thanking Him for His blessings.

—Jeffrey Unger

Jeffrey Unger is a native of Queens, New York. He is the managing director of Kalmon Dolgin Affiliates, Inc., a commercial real estate brokerage in Brooklyn and Queens.

Thank Heaven for Little Girls

"You're not my dad!" The fear of one day hearing those words was like cement poured and set in my brain, blocking any free-flowing thoughts about possibly adopting a child. After trying for five years to have a child of our own, my wife began thinking about adoption, but I wouldn't even consider it. I not only feared that my adopted child might rebel, but I also thought there was no way I could possibly love an adopted child as if he or she were of my own flesh and blood.

Despite her desperate desire to have children, my wife, Susan, was patient with me. She understood that my work as a sheriff's deputy somewhat abetted the hardening of my heart. So, rather than engage me in persuasive arguments about the subject, Susan simply asked me to pray that the Lord would soften my heart and that His will would be done. I obliged.

Before long, a light bulb turned on inside my head. It began to occur to me that I could love an adopted child as my own, and I reasoned that my parenting would make all the difference in how that child regarded Susan and me. Susan was delighted when I agreed to begin the adoption process, filling out paper work, and saving money. Then, the waiting began.

About six months later, the adoption agency called us to tell us they had an infant girl with respiratory problems. Her birth mother chose another family, but when that family heard about her medical condition, they declined, thinking they couldn't handle it. Following an emergency prayer meeting, the adoption agency staff decided that Susan and I would be best suited for the case. We had saved $16,000, but would need another $10,000 for medical expenses. So, we had to say, "No."

It was God's will that we have this little girl because almost immediately after Susan hung up with the agency, she received another phone call. It was Brenda, a woman with whom Susan worked at a chiropractic service. Even though she didn't know the woman very well, Susan began spilling her heart out over the devastation of having to turn away a needy infant. Brenda told Susan that the Lord had blessed her business and that she wanted to share the blessing with us by paying the additional $10,000! We didn't even know her last name.

Sadly, we learned that this woman who God sent to help us was killed in a car accident a few years later. She had made $3,000 worth of installments, and to this day we have no idea who picked up the remainder. We suspect the Christian director of the agency forgave our debt.

We named our daughter Hannah, after the prophet Samuel's mother who had been barren for so long. God answered Susan's prayers for a child just as He had answered Hannah's plea and gave her Samuel.

I fell in love with Hannah before I even met her. I was anxious to help her recuperate from neonatal surgery, and even more determined and prayerful when the doctor told us that she might never be able to speak. A day after she was born, Hannah had emergency surgery to open her esophagus, which was not attached to her stomach. During the process her vocal cords were paralyzed.

We first saw Hannah in the neonatal intensive care unit when she was three days old. Passing by the hospital's nursery, I could hear the cry of newborns through the thick glass, but when I reached the NICU, there was our little Hannah with all the facial expressions of a crying infant, yet not a sound to be heard. It was heart wrenching! "If only my little girl could have my vocal cords," I thought. I loved her more than I ever would have imagined I could, and I would do whatever was necessary to help her live a normal life.

Three weeks later, Hannah was home and we were feeding her through a tube in her nose. Day by day, our baby was getting stronger. During preparation for a second surgery, doctors saw some promise that Hannah's nerves might rejuvenate, so they held off on the procedure. Little by little, as months passed, Hannah started making weak sounds. By the time she was one, she was as noisy as any other one-year-old. All Susan and I could do was thank God for this miracle. We were a complete family, and our little angel was going to be fine.

Being of modest means, a second adoption was not even a consideration. So, when Hannah began asking Susan for a sister, we dismissed the request as "typical toddler behavior." We figured it would pass. However, when Hannah was about four we stood outside her bedroom door one night and overheard her praying, "Thank you, God, for the baby sister you're gonna send me." At that point we began to wonder, "Could we adopt another child?"

The deal was sealed when we were visiting friends who had an adopted a girl from China. Their daughter, who was two years old and barely knew me, immediately crawled up under my arm and sat on my lap. She looked up at me with her huge brown eyes and smiled. Her sweet face melted my heart. Within two months, we began the process of Chinese adoption.

Six months later, we went to China to pick up our second daughter, eleven-month-old Olivia. Olivia had the good fortune of spending her first months of life with wonderful foster parents, with whom we stay in contact. We consider them Olivia's grandparents. They've been able to watch her grow through video mail and infrequent visits. Two years later, we adopted Julianna.

Susan had since taken a job with Great Wall China Adoption to help families like ours realize their dreams. Our hearts broke for Julianna, who had been languishing since birth in an orphanage. Julianna became part of our family when she was ten months old. To our surprise, her two older sisters tenderly accepted her.

Because she sees all kinds of special needs cases, Susan began to question whether we could do more to help Chinese orphans. Could we afford it? Would we be able to handle a "special needs" child with three other children? These and other questions pervaded our thoughts. We had numerous discussions about it and spoke with our parents as well. Finally, we put it in the Lord's hands. We prayed, "God, please shut the door if enough is enough," but the door kept opening wider!

We adopted Isabella from China when she was three-and-a-half, the same age as Julianna. Isabella is considered "special needs" because of a red blood cell disorder called thalassemia. We did our homework and legwork prior to adopting Isabella to make sure we understood the severity of her case. Isabella has certain dietary restrictions, needs constant monitoring, and may need future blood transfusions, but other than tiring a bit more easily than most, she is quite normal.

To simply say Susan and I have been blessed with four daughters would mitigate the impact of the Lord's grace upon us. Quite frankly, we've been showered with blessings from the time I began to pray that the Lord would soften my heart to adoption.

Overseas adoption is costly, but each time the Lord paved the way. My in-laws assisted us with the adoption of Olivia. The combination of a home equity loan and tax refund enabled us to adopt Julianna. However, when the opportunity arose to adopt Isabella, we weren't sure how we'd pay for it. We decided to put a piece of land on the market. We weren't sure it would sell, but again we deferred to God. No one haggled over the price, and we used that sale to pay for our third Chinese adoption.

Our lives are hectic but fun. Susan still works for Great Wall China Adoption and I accompany her on Q&A workshops where I share my experience with men who are tentative about adopting. My message is two-fold: the bond between a father and his adopted children is as strong as any father's; and I am living proof that it is in giving that we receive.

—Art Fremer

Art Fremer was born and raised on Long Island, New York. He now lives in Florida with his wife of sixteen years, Susan, and their four daughters. A sergeant with the Pasco County Sheriff's office, Art oversees the Community Policing Unit. He loves the outdoors, especially fishing, boating, and camping. Art was a big Tampa Bay Lightning fan prior to their 2004 Stanley Cup victory, and he's a diehard Pittsburgh Steelers football enthusiast. Like many Americans, he and Susan keep Starbucks in business.

Acknowledgments

Many thanks to:

- All the fathers who shared their faith and hope, their joys and struggles of fatherhood with us and our readers.

- Lorraine Ranalli for her creative and insightful contributions to several of the stories.

- *Women's Word* magazine and *Christianity Today* for sharing several of their stories with us.

- George Abbott for his wonderful cartoons.

- Kinsey Caruth for his cover design.

- Annamarie Adkins, Elena Perri, Michael Flickinger, and Michael Fontecchio for their editorial and technical assistance.

Jeff Cavins, Matthew Pinto,
Mark Armstrong, and Patti Maguire Armstrong

Editor and Contributor Contact Information

To contact one of the contributors, please write them at the following address:

(Name of writer)
c/o Ascension Press
P.O. Box 1990
West Chester, PA 19380

Or by e-mail:
AmazingGrace@ascensionpress.com

To contact one of the co-editors, please write them at one of the following addresses:

Jeff Cavins
P.O. Box 1533
Maple Grove, MN 55311
Or at: jcavins@attbi.com

Matthew Pinto
P.O. Box 1990
West Chester, PA 19380
Or at: mpinto@ascensionpress.com

Mark and Patti Armstrong
P.O. Box 1532
Bismarck, ND 58502
Or at: armstrong@bis.midco.net
www.RaisingCatholicKids.com

About the Editors

Jeff Cavins served as a Protestant minister for twelve years before returning to the Catholic faith. His story is chronicled in his autobiography, *My Life on the Rock* (Ascension Press, 2001). Jeff is best-known as the founding host of the popular EWTN television program *Life on the Rock* and is the author of *I'm Not Being Fed!* (Ascension Press, 2005). With Matthew Pinto, he is the co-creator of the *Amazing Grace* series. He is also the creator and principal author of *The Great Adventure*, a popular Bible study program. Jeff and his wife, Emily, reside in Minnesota with their three daughters.

Matthew Pinto is the author of the best-selling question-and-answer book *Did Adam & Eve Have Belly Buttons?* (Ascension Press, 1998), co-author (with Jason Evert) of *Did Jesus Have a Last Name?* (Ascension Press, 2005), and co-creator of the *Friendly Defenders Catholic Flash Cards* series. Matt is co-founder of several Catholic organizations, including CatholicExchange.com and *Envoy* magazine, and the creator, with Jeff Cavins, of the *Amazing Grace* series. Matt and his wife, Maryanne, live in Pennsylvania with their five sons.

Mark Armstrong lives in North Dakota with his wife, Patti, and their family. After spending nearly thirty years as an awarding-winning broadcast journalist, Mark currently serves as the communications executive for Workforce Safety & Insurance. Mark and Patti speak both individually on Catholic topics and as a couple on their marriage conversion. Mark also uses a missionary image of Our Lady of Guadualupe to tell the story of St. Juan Diego and the parallels between our modern age and the Aztec culture.

Patti Maguire Armstrong is the mother of ten children, including two adopted AIDS orphans from Kenya. She worked in the fields of social work and public administration before staying home full-time to raise her children. As a freelance writer, Patti has published more than 400 articles for both secular and religious publications. She has authored the book *Catholic Truths for Our Children* (www.scepterpublishers.org) as a guide to help parents pass on the Catholic faith, and serves as co-editor of the *Amazing Grace* series.